SHE WAS MY MOTHER

Strong and determined, she would organise us all into the perfect assembly line. There were 8 hours and 2000 mutton rolls to be made for the charity event that night.

The freshly made pancakes that would form the outer crust were still setting. Blocks of meat still needed to be cut into thousands of cubes, and the breadcrumbs had some time to go before they would be golden-brown. She would move smoothly between it all, knowing where everything was, what was needed, and exactly how it needed to be done.

Though she was a socialite at heart, she also understood the task at hand and focused on getting it done. She worked so fast, her hands would move at a speed like no other – no one could keep up!

I can still hear the chattering women (her voice of course being the loudest) as they congregated in the makeshift kitchen that was our garage. They shared a desire to do whatever they could to help those who did not have the opportunities that they did.

I remember how they crafted each roll meticulously so it would not unravel when dipped into the boiling oil. She would remind us that food prepared in service of others, must be even better than that we would eat ourselves.

The kids would line up against the bench, fixated on her every instruction, eager to impress but cheekily sneaking a taste whenever we got the chance. She was kind but relentless; if we were given a task, we knew to do it well or not at all.

As time ticked on, the kitchen became more chaotic – pots banged, oil crackled, Dad ran behind us with his washcloth.

This is how we grew up. Surrounded by the chaos and vibrancy of food, prepared in the service of others.

Years would pass, and as she settled into her new home in Australia, her service to others would grow. She was doing what she could, in gratitude for the life that was given to her.

What made her truly powerful was her resilience, which was laced with an unwavering belief that doing something was better than doing nothing, and that in some small way her efforts could make the world a better place.

She never tired. She never gave up.

She was amazing. She was my mother.

Jaiyanthi Suthanthiraraj, 1956–2015

Because you were, we are.
Let your spirit continue to brighten the world.

Abarna Suthanthiraraj

HOW THIS BOOK CAME TO BE

In her final year as the book was coming together, my mother would always ask "How are the recipes tasting?" and "When will I see the book?"

Now, finally, the cookbook is here. It is a testament to the women whose food nourishes and whose resilience inspires; and to you who encouraged these stories to be told. We hope these stories inspire and generate rich new experiences and we hope this book makes you proud.

Each time I come to Sri Lanka with Palmera, I meet these amazing women – I see their strength in things they may never notice. How they cook from scratch, with just a few utensils, how they manage to pay the bills and feed their children, even when there is little money coming in; how they somehow keep their family together, despite the many hardships they endure.

When I share my admiration for them, they giggle. They are shy to hear themselves revered in this way because they don't see their strength as I do. You see, in this part of the world this is how they survive. They don't see themselves as any different from their neighbours, so how can they say they are strong?

As you enter their houses, the first thing they do is offer you a simple lime drink, or get you some biscuits. And then they ask you to stay for lunch.

Food is their life and a language they are at ease with. So what better way to tell their story than through food?

Witnessing this in each woman, inspires me, makes me stronger, and I wanted to share their story more widely. They possess a strength and a resilience so beautiful, so pure and yet so humble, that it cannot but inspire.

With this idea, incubated over the years of knowing the women through their journeys with Palmera, this cookbook was born. We didn't have a grand plan – it grew organically. In encountering the women's stories, we, each of us, brought something of ourselves to its telling.

TRADITION

In their kitchens, Abhi and Shobi sat with the women, sharing in the cooking, eating and laughing. The stories flowed. They were momentary encounters with rich traditions that reached back many generations. The stories were gathered, an inscription for each dish of joy, sadness or a hint of nostalgia.

"We long for the days we can cook the great dishes our mothers made us, the variety of snacks we grew up with. We long to be able to make all these foods at home and teach these dishes to our children."

Many of these women had never written down a recipe before, so who better than Nesa Aunty, author of *Recipes of the Jaffna Tamils*, to put together the missing pieces so that we could present these traditional recipes here.

PLAY AND LOVE

Pat, Ramya, Fabio and Tharindu captured images of the food and of its preparation. The women loved to see these photos. They would look at the screen and laugh, never having seen photos of themselves in the kitchen – what joy!

They also captured images of love and tenderness against the vibrant village landscape.

"I used to buy most of my foods from shops but my husband refused to do this and insisted on teaching me how to cook … He knew I enjoyed buying food out and sometimes he made food and wrapped it in parcels to make it seem as though he had bought it from outside."

RESILIENCE

All the interviews were conducted in the women's mother-tongue, Tamil. The conversations were free-flowing going to places of deep sadness, but also illustrating their strength in overcoming their circumstances.

So we ended up with many hours of footage. Srethanya, Logi Aunty, Sambavi, Sagar and Saon Uncle sieved through it all, translating and recording the powerful stories.

NOURISHMENT AND WELLBEING

With these stories our amazing Anjali began her crafting. She brought the book together – ensuring the integrity of each story. Working so intensely with the stories and the recipes inspired in her a new way of looking at food – of the joy and happiness it could bring, as well as the nourishment.

"The kitchen symbolises a place of joy where I can cook and provide the things my children love to eat."

The content was then edited by Jessica, Fiona, Karen and Erin.

OPTIMISM

We then had our test kitchen of over 25 people including Angie, Ashika, Aswini, Caroline, Danu, Devi Aunty, Diana Aunty, Gionata, Girija Aunty, Janani, Karthik, Logika, Manohari Aunty, Nandini Aunty, Niv, Thiru Uncle, Priya, Ravi Aunty, Riona, Shamim Aunty, Sivashna, Sudath, Talitha and Tammy Aunty try out each recipe for us.

Food photographers Suja, Emily-May, Shelley and Styliani, with the help of our decorator, Shaminie, captured the final dish.

It was an incredible process to observe these dishes being recreated, some of them by people who had never tried anything like it before and other times by people who had last eaten the dish as a child. Already, the dreams of the women, that others continue the traditions of their food seemed to be coming true.

The book's narrative was then charted with Manjula Aunty on her long, wooden dining table over a couple of mornings, and kneaded together by Jess. How best to order the content, to hold onto the potency of these stories and yet present them to the world to be heard and experienced?

RESOURCEFULNESS

Shruti and Frank of Pink Tank Creative worked with us from the beginning.

Inspired by images and stories of the women, to present the book in the most visually powerful, authentic and cook-friendly way, theirs is like the enterprising and resourceful spirit of the women themselves.

Siv ensured the manuscript of words and images on our screens took form in the book you are holding. Thanks to her it is in bookshops, homes and warming kitchens and bellies around the world!

Of course, this was all only possible because of the amazing women of TEWO, who raised funds through cooking and other events to produce this book. Their commitment, passion and entrepreneurial spirit continues to inspire us.

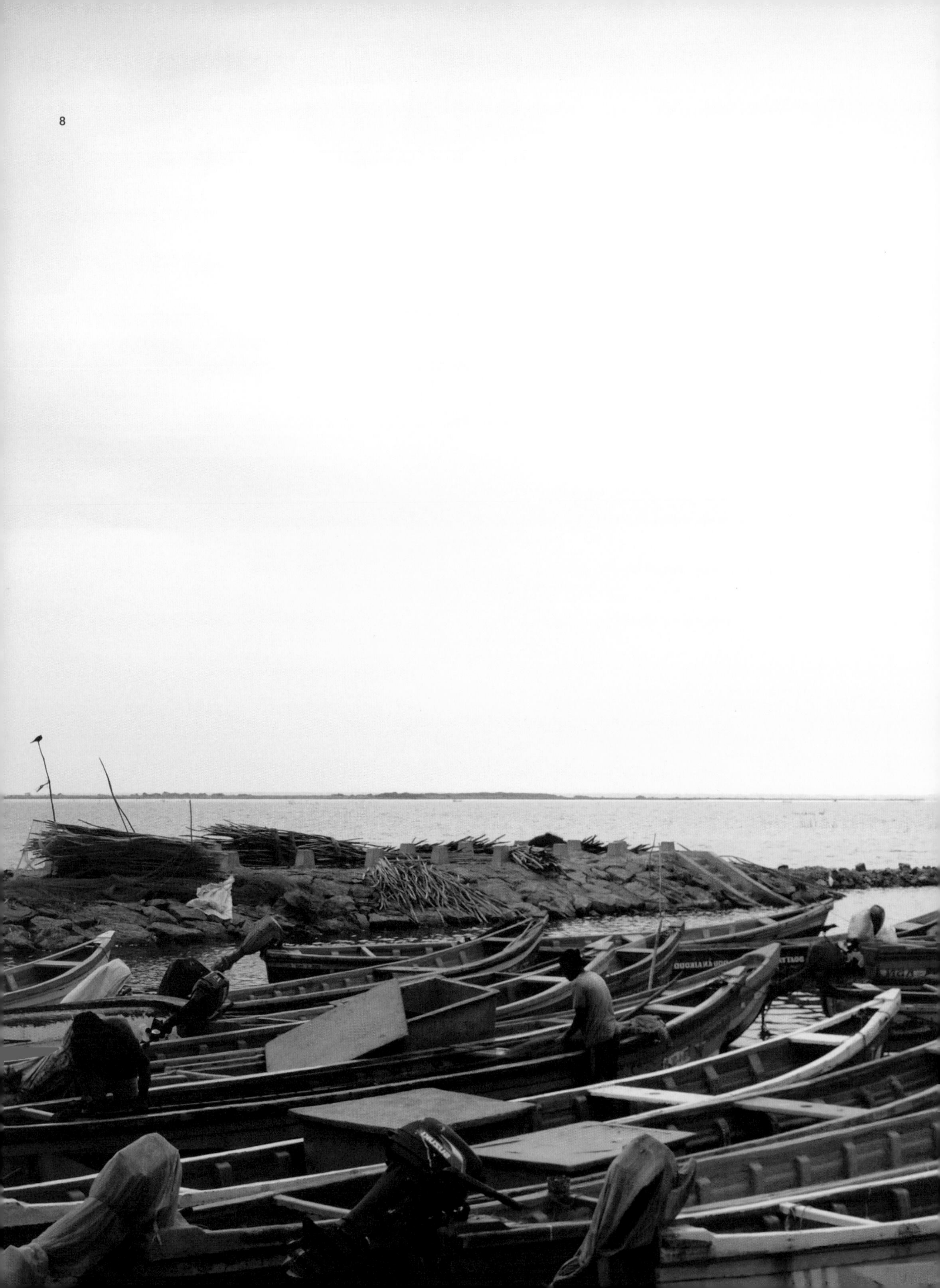

You see, nearly everyone here was a volunteer and there are so many more names and faces we haven't even shared — of the women, of the local partner organisations, and others.

ALL WHO HAVE WORKED ON THE BOOK HAVE GIVEN OF THEMSELVES AND IN DOING SO KNOWINGLY OR UNKNOWINGLY, HIGHLIGHTED WHAT THIS BOOK IS TRYING TO SHOWCASE: THE POWER OF TRADITION, A PLAYFULNESS AND LOVE EVEN IN ADVERSITY, AN INNER STRENGTH AND RESILIENCE, A DEEP AND ALMOST INNATE KNOWING OF THE NEED FOR NOURISHMENT, AN EVER-PRESENT OPTIMISM AND A FEISTY RESOURCEFULNESS.

This is the first time Palmera has pulled together a book like this and we hope it inspires you as it has us. It really has been an effort of like-minded people coming together, united by one purpose — to tell the powerful stories of women.

"ELLAAM ORU KELVI VIDIUM ILLAI, IRULUM ILLAI." EVERYTHING IN OUR LIFE IS UNCERTAIN. WE NEITHER HAVE LIGHT NOR DARKNESS IN OUR LIVES.

In the shady grove of trees, amongst the mango and murungakkai, she sits peeling the roots of the palmyra. Brown, coarse and weathered on the outside; inside, creamy white fibres are firm to the touch. They are tough, unbreakable and resilient.

———————————————

AS YOU ENTER HER KITCHEN,

the air is thick with the aroma of food. It is a combination of the dishes she has prepared on other days and the anticipation of what she is about to conjure today.

The kitchen is equipped roughly, but there are splashes of colour. Shiny, red plastic containers, a brightly patterned tablecloth – white flowers against a sky-blue background – and little teddy bears in the window. The utensils are worn, a dark layer at their base silently conveying all the time spent on the wood fire. The smooth, textured brown inside speaks of the many meals before.

Ayini smiles, welcoming you with her eyes. Her bright pink dress has white spots, small and large, with magenta flowers scattered generously. "*Sollunga*," she says: "*Tell me.*"

Next to the fire, everything is intensified: the smoke, the heat, the orange flame, flying sparks and the sounds of water hissing. Her presence seems to tame the fire.

On the kitchen bench, ingredients present themselves in their raw form a whole coconut awaiting grating into pure white, cream-filled shreds, sumptuous in their promise of thick milk; seeds she will grind to a paste on the black stone mortar; and the beans and tapioca, few in number till they are dissected into small cubes, and magically grow in volume.

The mud house is dark and cool in the sweltering heat. Most of the cooking is done outside, during daylight hours, since electricity is scarce.

Soon the hollow of the kitchen is filled with a myriad of sounds: crackling, pounding, stirring, clanging and chatter. Ayini has started to cook. There is conversation as people pass through: children, a relative or two, some furtively taking a bit. She becomes annoyed for she may have to prepare more, but she is also happy that her food is being eaten. The sounds of music filter through.

Here in the kitchen, Ayini is in complete control. She creates sustenance from the meagre ingredients available to her. She wields her power with certainty and calm. Food, after all, is the first need.

Through the difficulties and displacement of the last few decades, she has responded to this need. Her chef's hat has been replaced by that of a magician – artfully substituting rice flour with the oversupply of lentils, adding some extra chilli to make up for the lack of ginger, adding water so it lasts longer and, at times, skipping her own meal when there is not enough.

"Even when we had the necessary ingredients, many of us were not in the mood to make it. Because of the long preparation times and the uncertainty of what would happen next or where we'd be tomorrow, we often didn't cook."

But there is no show. Behind her humility is unseen courage and strength. She adds these to her cauldron and it is these qualities, combined with the food, that have kept her family alive.

Her smile is playful, her eyes self-assured and focused. She is unaffected by your presence, except for her smile and the few words she utters. She clears a small space on the deep red floor and sits down to grate the coconut. She scrapes it over a protruding circular grate, over and over, until the morsels of white coconut grow into a substantial mound.

Her hands work like a dancer's *mudras* (hand gestures), turning, shaping, scooping, deliberately and deftly. The creases on her fingers deepen with each rotation of the coconut shell, opening and closing to reveal the softness and lightness of her palms. Her stories lie in these crevices – scripts of tradition, childhood memories and of deep sorrow.

Of once knowing the abundance of fresh eggs on a farm, to having to make do with whatever came from a nondescript time and place. Of not being able to provide her daughter with the food she needed, that is – a diet rich in protein and iron, designed to support a young woman's body through the changes of puberty.

Her daughter Kavya enters the kitchen. She stops briefly to see what her mother is doing. Kavya takes over for a bit, under her mother's guidance. There is a delicateness, a reverence as she teaches her daughter. "Kavya's a good girl," she says. "Now we need to revive the practices of our ancestors and eat their traditional foods."

As her hands settle back into the comfort of this well-known routine, they begin to take over. This ritual of grating the coconut, performed in so many circumstances, before, during and, now, after the war – who would have thought it would become a sort of lifeline for each family? So many occasions, so many dishes.

Each time, the circumstance is slightly different. It is through the rituals of preparation and cooking that she recalls, lives and heals.

And then you gradually begin to take in what she is preparing.

She takes flour and mixes it with water. She adds some of the delicate milk she has squeezed from the gratings of the coconut. She mixes the light, pale red dough and then spoons it into a wooden press.

The press looks worn but reliable, its lines and patches of dark and light a record of its encounters with many batters in her hands. There are cracks in the arms of the press in the direction of the wood grain. They are an indication of its age, its perpetual cycling between moisture and dryness. Each time the wood ends up a little drier, exposing itself a little more.

From the thick dough, which she forces down into the press, a mass of thin noodles emerge, multiplying. They sit delicately, light noodle pancakes waiting patiently as more are pushed out.

The *idiappam* each await their turn to steam in an aluminium vessel. After a number of steam cycles, enough are accumulated to satiate the family. They will be paired with a smooth, warm vegetable curry of coconut milk, and lashings of spices. This combination of a flour-based staple like *idiappam* with a curry, is a common meal here.

Though the meal's form has remained unchanged for years, the food embodies memories from significant times in her life. The time it tasted odd because she had no fresh garlic, or the moment when the *appam* was left over and she realised Vinay may not come back; or when Savi first joined them, and became part of their family.

The aroma of what she has cooked fills the house, drifting beyond its walls. Its warmth and freshness is inviting. What promise it holds, a celebration of the present, a reason to fully occupy this moment.

The adults in the house stay close, waiting until all the meal's components are ready and assembled. This is the power of food: to draw together, to warm from the inside, to nourish and to strengthen with the momentary exclusion of all else.

She calls out. The children and adults gather on the floor of the kitchen. They are her impatient muse and audience in one. They eagerly await and then savour what she serves them. Steaming, fluffy idiappam with a pungent murungakkai curry spooned over the top.

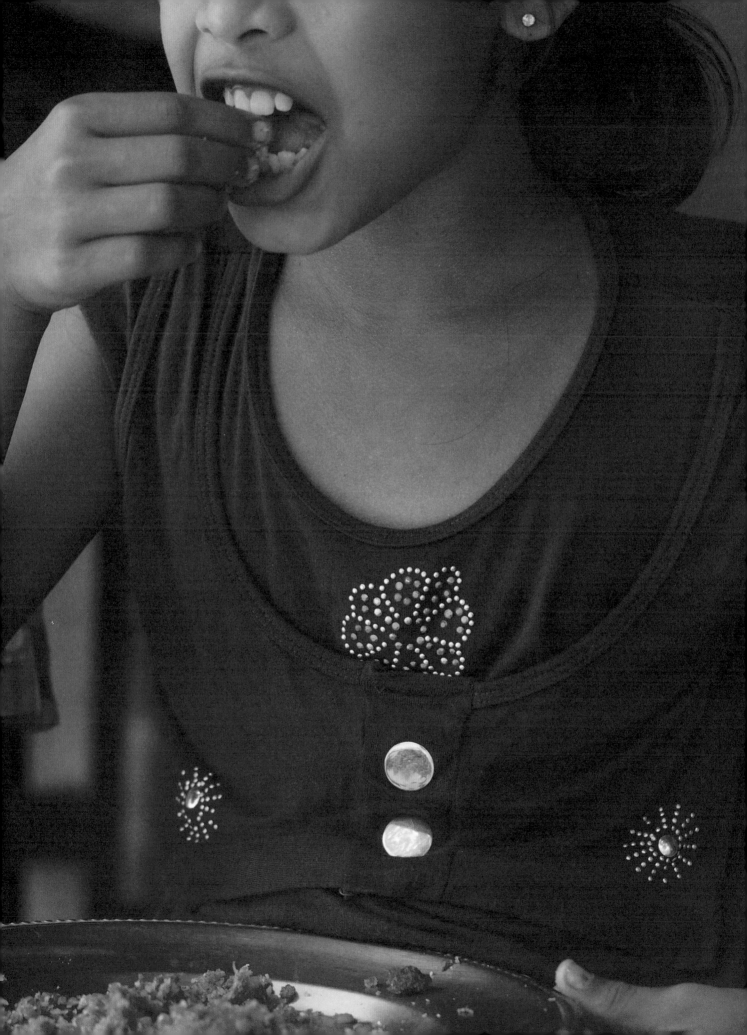

For the little ones, she mixes the food herself into little balls – playthings they eagerly swallow from her hand. When they have had their fill and are impatient to get up, she threatens. They resume their receiving positions.

You wonder what happened to this food – the staple, the festive and the sacred – in the tough times. Amidst the ongoing violence and its continuous assault on the senses, you imagine the experience of food might be heightened; its taste savoured more deeply and the very act of eating becoming a form of resistance.

Even as families were displaced – from staying in a relative's house, to camping under a tree or staying in safe houses, to finally being in the refugee camps – women would instantly devise ways to cook and feed their families, ushering in a semblance of normality.

It was as if she converted an unwavering, intangible inner strength into tangible nourishment. And where she could not, she would exchange what she had, usually rice, lentils and flour, for the elixirs and medicines that she needed.

This story of survival is narrated by each woman. Its many versions form this book. It is a story that exists in the everyday, and that has extended over many years. It is inspiring to us, quite unremarkable to her. It is the story of a strength generated within, in response to outside challenges, and therein lies its power to inspire us, who are largely free to choose our challenges.

In the food you taste there is much more than just the flavours. Now, there is a lightness and hope, a lushness in the thick curry.

Will the children drink *kool* in the month of Aadi and eat *panang katti* (palmyra sugar), as the song says? Will *uluththang kali* (black gram cream) again be prepared to celebrate a young woman's coming of age? It seems that the traditions of food are again emerging, and in turn, renewing and anchoring communities around them.

AS AYINI AND THE OTHERS REBUILD THEIR LIVES IN NEW DWELLINGS, THE FOUNDATION CONTINUES TO BE FOOD.

Now, however, the challenges are different. The cost of food has risen sharply due to the prevailing drought. Many women who used to rely on their husbands to cultivate the land, are now the heads of their households and must secure an income for their family. With the additional responsibility, they can no longer afford the time to prepare nutritious food.

"We used to have three or four curries every meal… it's not like that anymore. Now we just look for the easiest things to prepare and that's what we make."

Palmera is working with these women to help build new lives – lives where they are in control of their own destiny.

We share a common belief that the best way out of aid and poverty is by creating economic self-sufficiency. Without it, there is no freedom or opportunity. With it, there is choice and dignity.

We are focused on creating economic opportunities, which provide an alternative to the cycle of aid, dependence and poverty. In this narrative, women are dreaming up new and powerful ways to exist and lead` their communities.

Through village-based micro-enterprises, these women now wear another hat: they are entrepreneurs and village leaders. They have a voice and make decisions about their future. In a village in the district of Vavuniya, Palmera is working with farmers to grow papayas for export. With training in business, horticulture and water management they are successfully generating an income: *"We are learning new things, learning how to sell to the outside world. We need to change our traditional techniques but we are learning and we will get there. It is important for our future."*

In imagining a new future for herself and her family, Ayini dreams of an abundance of food, of an affordable supply of fresh vegetables, of mounds of spices, and of foods cooked not only to survive, but to celebrate life.

"I grow my own vegetable crops and have my own vayal (paddy field). Because of this I only need to buy fish to feed my children. I sow the paddy five times a year and am able to convert the harvest into rice or grind it to make rice flour, saving me money. I also earn a living by selling some of the rice I harvest."

But it is not simply a return to the idyll of what once was. As she begins to engage with community projects – learning, understanding and growing to rely on herself to generate an income – she is crafting a new way of existing, a way in which the next generation can fly and, perhaps, where she can too. *"We live in the hope that our children will be able to make a living for themselves."*

This book illuminates stories of the everyday, of the rituals and lives of 34 women across the north and east of Sri Lanka. We see life through their eyes, and in their challenges of survival we see our own.

The stories are distinct compositions, but also variations on a theme of strength, creativity and resilience. It is through the recipes that we witness these women's stories and recall their spirit. By recreating their recipes we pay homage to the traditions they have kept alive and their improvisations in the name of survival.

"Where there is sea, there are waves, winds, fish, crabs and so on. Similarly, in our lives we have problems, sorrow, happiness, we have everything, but they are all part and parcel of life and make our lives what they are. Our skills lie in facing and overcoming these issues and moving forward."

This book brings us closer to women we may never know. Women who are brave and have a story worth telling, through food worth sharing.

Anjali Roberts

THE BASICS

UTENSILS

A   Mortar and pestle (ural)
B   Thosai pan (thosai kalu)
C   Murukku press in brass (murukku ural)
D   Rice winnowing tray (soolahu) and
    sifting bowl (arikkan chatti)
E   Kundu thosai mould (kuli paniyaram)
F   Coconut shell spoon (siratte aheppe)
G   Idli steamer trays (idli thattu)
    and pot (chatti)
H   Idiappam press in wood (idiappam ural)
I   Metal wok and lid (iramb chatti)
J   Idiappam steamer pot lid
K   Murukku press in wood (murukku ural)
L   Puttu steamer (puttu kullal)

C

G

LENTILS

A   Split yellow lentil (kadalai parrupu)

B   Chickpeas (kadalai)

C   Split black gram (ulunththu)

D   Masoor dhal (maisoor parrupu)

E   Yellow skinless split mung dhal

F   Green gram (paasipayaru)

G   Skinless split black gram

RICE

A   Long grain (basmati) rice
B   Red rice
C   Idli rice
D   Broken rice
E   Samba rice

THE KITCHEN SYMBOLISES A PLACE OF JOY WHERE I CAN COOK AND PROVIDE THE THINGS MY CHILDREN LOVE TO EAT. IT BRINGS ME GREAT HAPPINESS TO WATCH MY CHILDREN EAT. I AM ALSO AFRAID OF FEEDING MY CHILDREN FOOD FROM SHOPS, I DON'T KNOW WHAT INGREDIENTS ARE USED. I FEEL I CAN PROVIDE MORE NUTRITION THROUGH MY OWN COOKING.

SNACKS

Kaarai Kaaju

Maravalli Poriyal

Murukku

Kadalai Vadai

Paruththithurai Vadai

Keerai Vadai

Iraal Vadai

Veppam-poo Vadaham

Kadalai Sundal

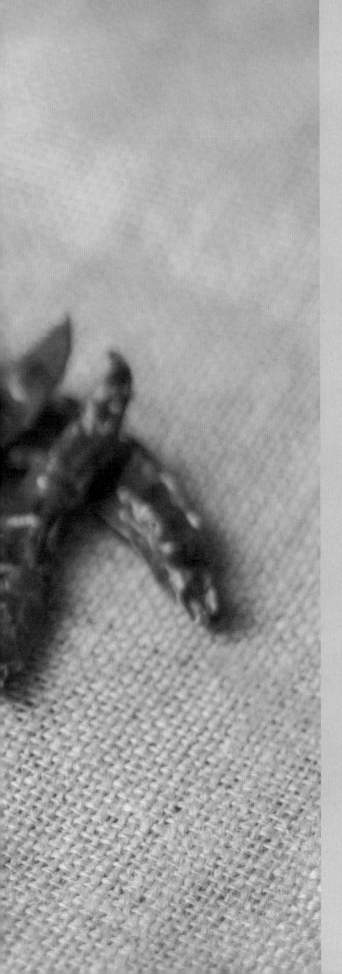

KAARAI KAAJU

Chilli Cashew Nuts /

The humble cashew, rich and creamy, is given an epicurean treatment. Roasted, then spiced, this is a celebration of the everyday.

COOKING TIME: 10 MIN
SERVINGS: 8-10

INGREDIENTS

200 g raw cashew nuts

1 tbsp oil, sesame (gingelly) or coconut oil

1 tsp salt (or to taste)

1 tsp ground pepper

1 tsp chilli powder

METHOD

1. Heat oil in frying pan. When hot, add cashew nuts and fry until they turn a light golden colour.
2. Remove cashew nuts and place in a bowl.
3. Add salt, pepper and chilli powder. Mix well.
4. Serve.

Cassava Chips / *Fresh, crisp, spicy cassava chips are eaten on their own or paired with a simple rice and curry. These chips add a burst of texture and spice to any eating experience.*

MARAVALLI PORIYAL

PREPARATION TIME: 25 MIN
COOKING TIME: 15 MIN
SERVINGS: 5-6

INGREDIENTS

2 cassava roots (frozen roots can be used)

1 tsp chilli powder

½ tsp salt (or to taste)

Oil for deep-frying

METHOD

1. Peel cassava roots and wash well. Slice thinly.
2. In a bowl, mix cassava slices, chilli powder and salt. Set aside for 15 minutes.
3. Heat oil over medium-high heat. Deep-fry chips. Place chips on absorbent paper.
4. Serve warm or store in an airtight container until ready to be served.

CRUNCHY, COMFORTING MURUKKU

Vandana laments that her two children are missing out on the snacks she delighted in as a child. A fried, crunchy golden spiral of wheat flour, called *murukku*, was her favourite. Bite by bite, she would eat into the spiral until it was gone; then she would reach for another. *Murukku* was served at weddings, or simply stored in a jar at home, to be discovered in the hungry moments before dinner.

Remembering snacks like murukku, panangkali vaayppan (palmyra pulp fritter) and thothal (rice flour slice), brings a huge smile to Vandana's face. But now, even though she knows how to, her finances don't allow her to prepare these snacks. All that she can do is tell stories that make one's mouth water.

She longs for the day when she can recreate these heavenly snacks and continue a tradition that has been passed to her through many generations. She hopes that this book will help keep alive the recipes and the memories of foods that she feels fortunate to have inherited. And that one day, not only will she savour them again, but that her children and others around the world will discover the delights of *murukku*.

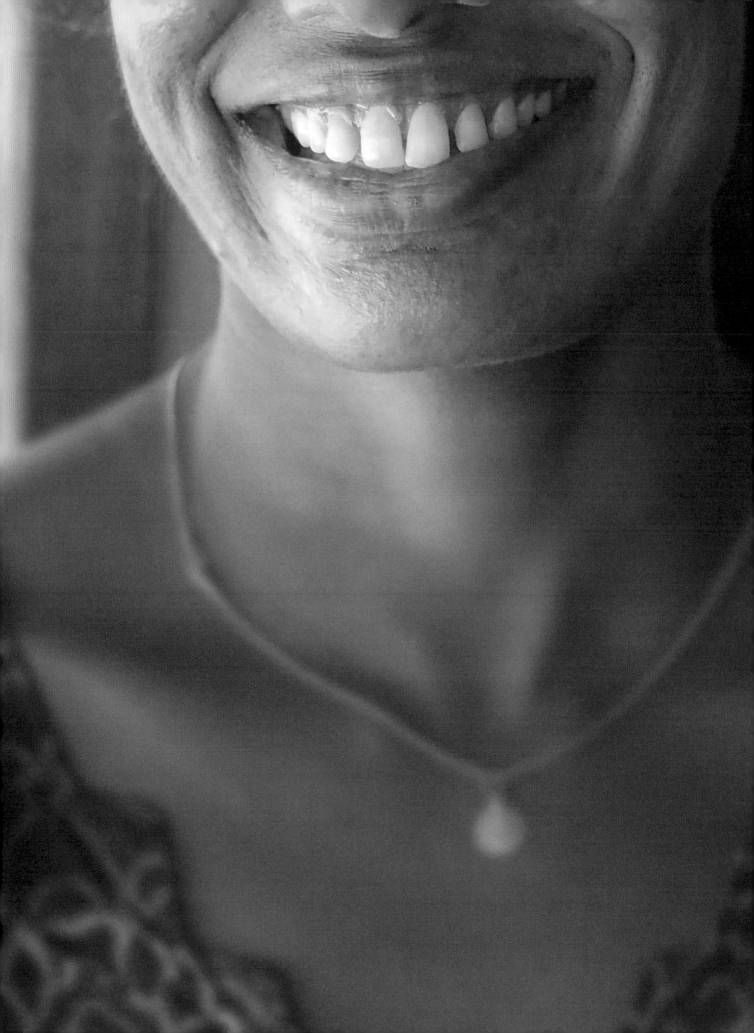

MURUKKU

Savoury Spiral Snacks / *Murukku presses used to be made of solid brass. Shiny and regal, all the family would take turns at squeezing out the mesmerising snake-like spirals. Murukku can be made out of many flours – rice, black gram, wheat or raagi. Its spiral forms are a delight to make and nibble on.*

PREPARATION TIME: 30 MIN
(+ STEAMING)
COOKING TIME: 15 MIN
MAKES: 15-20

INGREDIENTS

500 g plain flour (traditionally rice flour was used), steamed (see page 91)

½ tsp turmeric powder

¼ tsp ground pepper

1 tsp white sesame seeds

¼ tsp salt (or to taste)

Chilli powder (optional)

Hot water, as needed (around ¼ cup to begin with)

Oil for deep-frying

REQUIRED

» Murukku press
» Squares of newspaper or banana leaf, about palm-size

METHOD

1. Steam plain flour. Remove and set aside to cool in a bowl.
2. Add turmeric powder, ground pepper and sesame seeds to flour. Mix well.
3. Add hot water gradually, kneading flour into a firm dough. The dough should be able to hold its shape.
4. Fill murukku press with a handful of dough.
5. Heat oil for deep-frying.
6. Using the murukku press, squeeze dough out into spirals on the pieces of paper (or banana leaf).
7. When oil is hot, slowly slide murukku spirals into oil. Turn occasionally until murukkus turns golden.
8. Drain on a tray lined with absorbent paper.
9. Store in an airtight container until ready to be served.

LENTIL AS ANYTHING (AND EVERYTHING)

Janani lowers her head, almost reverently, as she reflects on the staple the yellow lentil has been in her life. A smile flickers at the corner of her mouth as she recalls her early teens when she learnt from her mother how to soak, then boil the lentils, and flavour them with a fried mixture of garlic, green chillies, onions and curry leaves. The making of this simple side-dish was entrusted to her and she took her responsibility seriously, serving it as an accompaniment to *puttu* or *idiappa* at breakfast, with rice and meat curry in the afternoon, or with *idli* or *thosai* at dinner.

Her voice becomes softer, as she stoically tells of how lentils grew to be more than a side-dish during her time in the camps. It was often the only food her family had. As a result, she became more creative. Her eyes come alive and her smile reappears as she remembers the first time she made her yellow lentil *vadais* in the camps: *"I soaked and ground the lentils and added a lot of spices like chilli and cumin. Then I rolled the mixture into small balls, which I fried in hot oil. I added these to rings of boiled onions and fried chillies for a snack. The leftover fried balls I transformed into a curry to create another meal. I also experimented with the ground yellow lentils and made thosais for a dinner treat."*

She ponders aloud about how resourceful she was with the over-supply of lentils through that time. Outside the camps she bartered the excess for fresh items like ginger and garlic. The novelty of these ingredients helped with her lentil experiments and enabled her to temporarily transport all of the family to another, more joyful world, outside of the camps.

Yellow Lentil Vadai / Moist yellow lentils are ground to a chunky paste, with bursts of curry leaf and shards of chilli. The disc-like vadais are deep-fried to a crisp outer shell around a fleshy, light inside.

KADALAI VADAI

PREPARATION TIME: 50 MIN
(+ SOAKING)
COOKING TIME: 30 MIN
MAKES: 30

INGREDIENTS

2 cups yellow lentils (kadalai parrupu), split and skinless, soaked for 2 hours

1 onion, chopped finely

¼ cup grated carrot (optional)

2 green chillies (or to taste), chopped finely

1 sprig curry leaves, chopped finely

¼ tsp salt (or to taste)

½ tsp chilli powder

Oil for deep-frying

METHOD

1. Drain lentils and grind to a coarse paste using a food processor or grinder.
2. Add onion, chillies, curry leaves, salt and chilli powder, and carrot (if using). Mix well.
3. Allow to stand for about 30 minutes.
4. To form each vadai, take a small ball of the mixture and shape into a disc of 3-4 cm diameter and 1-2 cm thickness.
5. Heat oil in a pan over medium-high heat.
6. Deep-fry the vadais, turning them over occasionally, until golden-brown.
7. Remove from oil and serve.

Spicy Flat Vadai /

The texture of this vadai is condensed from the traditional vadai and its flavours are concentrated in a more compact, crisp form. A mouthful of this wafer-thin snack yields intense flavours that simmer away on the palate. It is named after the village of Paruththithurai, which came to be called Point Pedro.

**PREPARATION TIME: 25 MIN
(+ SOAKING, STEAMING)
COOKING TIME: 30 MIN
MAKES: 20-30**

INGREDIENTS

1 cup black gram (ulunththu), skinless, soaked for 4 hours

2 cups plain flour

Salt (to taste)

Chilli flakes (to taste)

1 tbsp fennel seeds

1 sprig curry leaves, chopped finely

Water (as required)

Oil for deep-frying

METHOD

1. Steam 1 cup of plain flour (see page 91).
2. In a bowl, mix steamed plain flour and unsteamed plain flour.
3. Add salt, chilli flakes, fennel seeds and curry leaves. Mix well.
4. Drain soaked black gram and add to flour.
5. Mix into a dough, adding water a little at a time, so dough remains coarse and more dry than wet.
6. Form the dough into balls of 2-3 cm diameter and flatten with a rolling pin or by hand until they are approximately 2 mm thick. Use of a rolling pin will result in a flatter, more neat vadais.
7. Deep-fry in hot oil. When light golden, drain on absorbent paper. For a crisper texture, fry vadai until it is a deep golden colour.
8. Store in an airtight container until ready to be served.

PARUTHTHITHURAI VADAI

SNACKS ON THE RUN

Malathy would make spinach *vadais* as a side-dish to a meal – when she had time. She opens her palm to show how she would form the doughnut-shaped *vadais*, and then makes a finger-sized hole in the middle. She and her four children would also snack on them between meals. And when her husband returned home from a long day in the fields, the *vadais* would satiate his hunger and quell his impatience as he waited for Malathy to prepare dinner.

As she recalls events from the war and how the family moved from towns to forests and to the camps, her voice becomes whisper-quiet. She closes her eyes as she remembers the sky-high price of flour and the lack of cooking facilities. She disciplined herself to be more resourceful: the spinach *vadais* went from being a snack to their means of survival. She bartered flour for black gram (*ulunththu*) and ginger from other families, and sold her *vadais* on the streets, in the forest and the camps, so that she could feed her family.

She remembers the time she cooked a large batch of perfect, crispy, dough rings. She had just finished draining the oil off the rings, when shells began landing, some as close as 5 metres away. Quickly she abandoned her day's work to take shelter. When quiet descended, she emerged to find her perfect vadais covered in sand and shrapnel.

The next day, she exchanged flour again. This time she even made a *sambal* side with coconut and chillies to sell with the *vadais*.

INGREDIENTS

250 g black gram (ulunththu), split and skinless, soaked for at least 6 hours
1 green chilli, chopped finely
1 onion, chopped finely
7-8 curry leaves, chopped finely
¼ tsp chopped ginger
1 tsp salt
1 cup spinach, chopped finely
Oil for deep-frying
Banana leaves (optional), cut into palm-sized pieces, greased with ghee or oil, for sliding the *vadai* into the pan

METHOD

1. Drain black gram and grind to a fine paste using a food processor or grinder.
2. Add green chilli, onion, curry leaves, ginger, salt and chopped spinach. If using flour, add 1-2 cups of water. Mix well. The dough should be firm rather than runny or dry, and not sticky to the touch. Set aside for a few minutes.
3. Heat oil in a pan over medium-high heat.
4. Take a small ball of mixture and place it on a greased banana leaf. Gently flatten the ball and make a hole in the centre, like a doughnut.
5. Slide vadai into pan when oil is hot. Repeat the process.
6. Turn each vadai over until it is golden-brown.
7. Remove from oil and place on an absorbent surface. Serve warm.

PREPARATION TIME: 20 MIN (+ SOAKING)
COOKING TIME: 30 MIN
MAKES: 20

Spinach Vadai /

Fine ribbons of spinach weave through the fluffy white inside of this vadai, a variation on the traditional snack. Thick rings of dough are deep-fried in oil, until they turn golden-brown, with onions and spices lodged on their surface.

KEERAI VADAI

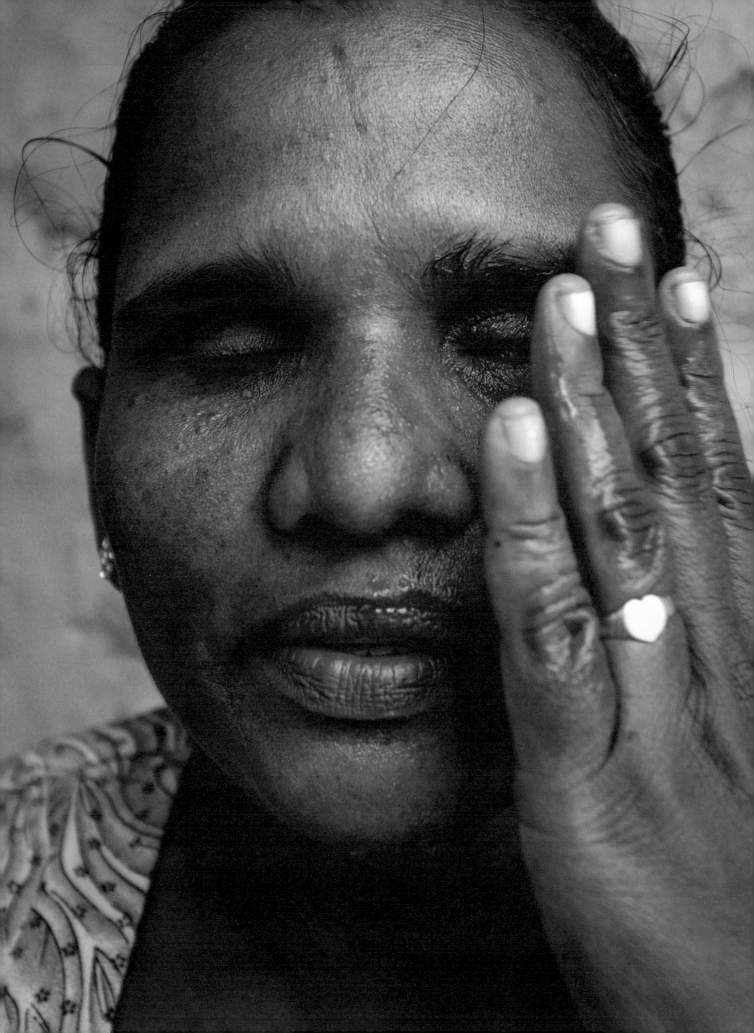

IT'S A REAL STRUGGLE AND BRINGS ME GREAT PAIN TO NOT BE ABLE TO PROVIDE OUR CHILDREN WITH THE FOODS THEY DESIRE, TO CONSTANTLY DENY THEM FOODS THEY WANT TO EAT.

Prawn Vadai / *Fresh prawns,
moist and fleshy, transform
the traditional vadai into
something that hints of the
sea and the street, of salt
and spice on balmy days.*

IRAAL VADAI

PREPARATION TIME: 35 MIN
(+ SOAKING)
COOKING TIME: 15 MIN
MAKES: 14-16

INGREDIENTS

2 cups yellow lentils (kadalai parrupu), split and skinless,
soaked for at least 2 hours

1 medium onion, chopped finely

1 cup whole, fresh prawns

2 green chillies, chopped finely

5-6 curry leaves, chopped finely

¼ tsp salt (or to taste)

½ tsp chilli powder

Oil for deep-frying

METHOD

1. Drain and grind yellow lentils to a coarse paste.
2. Shell and de-vein prawns. Rinse and dry.
3. In a mortar and pestle pound prawns into a paste.
4. Mix together all ingredients (except the oil).
5. Allow to stand for about half an hour.
6. Heat oil in a pan over medium-high heat.
7. Make little balls out of the mixture.
8. Deep-fry, turning occasionally until *vadais*
   are light brown.
9. Drain on absorbent paper.
10. Serve warm.

VEPPAM
THE MARGOSSA TREE

"Just sitting under the shade of this veppa maram is in itself so healthy,"
says Thiruchelvi, her 85-year-old face breaking into a satisfied sigh.
"If nothing else, we have health."

The *veppam* (margossa/neem) is tall and evergreen, another 'wonder tree'
tree found in almost every home in the village.

"My grandson is still taught to use the twig of the veppam tree to brush his teeth," Thiruchelvi
smiles, showing her own teeth which are still intact. *"It's not the nicest of tastes, quite bitter
actually, but its goodness far outweighs its bitter nature."* The oil from the *veppam* twig keeps
the gums and mouth healthy, fighting mouth ulcers and bad breath.

The leaves are crushed to extract the bitter *veppam-ennai* (neem oil). In traditional
ayurvedic, siddha and unani medicine, this oil has a multiple uses. It is anti-bacterial,
antiseptic and anti-fungal. The oil is extracted in myriad ways: hot water in which
veppam leaves are steeped is used as a wash in post-natal care; poultices made of
crushed *veppam* leaves are an anti-inflammatory, relieving the pain of swollen joints,
and the juice extracted from the leaves is used to purify the liver and reduce the
intensity of malarial fevers.

Skin conditions from boils to chicken pox and leprosy, are treated with a paste
of crushed *veppam* leaves. Patients are also given small bunches of leaves to brush
over their skin to quell incessant itchiness. Inside the rooms of the ill, bunches
of *veppam* leaves are hung to purify the air.

In the kitchen, the white flowers of the *veppam* tree are used to make *veppam-poo vadaham*,
a delicate fried snack. The leaves are stir-fried with other vegetables to mask
their bitterness.

*"My mother used to soak the leaves in young coconut water before cooking to rid them of
the bitterness in some way – but we still tasted its good bitterness!"* chuckles the
irrepressible Thiruchelvi.

The good bitterness is endlessly good it seems, from giving shade to cleaning the air,
and then healing from the inside out.

VEPPAM-POO VADAHAM

Margossa/Neem Flower Fry

The five delicate white petals of the margossa flower belie the bitterness of its tree. The flowers are dried, mixed with spices and lentil flour, and fried to a light crisp, to yield their goodness.

PREPARATION TIME: 30-40 MIN
(+ SOAKING)
COOKING TIME: 10 MIN
MAKES: 15-20

INGREDIENTS

3 cups margossa flowers (veppam-poo), cleaned and dried. Drumstick flowers (murunggai-poo) or lavender flowers can be substituted.

1 cup black gram (ulunththu) soaked for at least 2 hours

7 dried red chillies

2 tsp fennel seeds

1 tsp black peppercorns

Salt (to taste)

Oil for deep-frying

METHOD

1. Grind black gram coarsely and set aside.
2. Dry-roast fennel seeds and peppercorns. Remove from heat.
3. Grind or pound fennel seeds, peppercorns and dried chillies.
4. In a bowl, mix ground black gram, ground spices and margossa flowers. Add salt to taste. Mix well.
5. Form small, flat rounds of mixture, about 5-6 cm in diameter.
6. Place on a tray and dry in the oven at 80°C for 2 hours. Traditionally the vadaham mixture would be dried over a cloth in the sun for 4-6 days.
7. Store in an airtight container.
8. Deep-fry just before serving.

Vadahams are a popular savoury side-dish that vie with *pappadum* in a Sri Lankan meal. They can be made from many seasonal vegetables. Dried in the sun, these little tit-bits are kept in airtight containers till needed. They are then fried to make a nutritious, tasty accompaniment to a meal.

KADALAI SUNDAL

Stir-fried Chickpeas /

Full, fluffy chickpeas are coated in light coconut oil in the refreshing company of green mango, and grounded in a base of onion and chilli.

Sundals are savoury snacks.
"*They may be eaten to pass the time,*" says Maheswary, meaning they are made when people are together and wish to eat a small snack. Chickpea *sundal*, without the mango is a popular temple *prasatham* (an offering to the deity, which is then distributed among worshippers).

PREPARATION TIME: 30 MIN (+ SOAKING)
COOKING TIME: 1 HR
SERVINGS: 4-6

INGREDIENTS

500 g chickpeas, soaked overnight

2 tbsp oil, sesame (gingelly) or coconut oil

8-10 small rose onions or 2-3 shallots, sliced finely

5 dried red chillies, broken into pieces

½ cup green mango, chopped (optional)

½ tsp chilli powder

Water (to cover chickpeas in pot)

½ tsp salt

1 medium onion, chopped finely

METHOD

1. Drain chickpeas and rinse in cold water.
2. Heat oil in a pot. Add sliced rose onions or shallots and red chillies and sauté till onions are translucent.
3. Add chickpeas to pot, with chilli powder and salt. Cover with water.
4. Cover and cook till tender.
5. Remove from heat when cooked. Add chopped onions and mango bits.
6. Mix thoroughly and serve.

Maangai Oorugai

Thakkaali Yaam

Thengai-poo Sambal

Panang-kilangu Thuvaiyal

Thakkaali Sothi

Koththamalli Rasam

JAMS AND SIDES

MAANGAI OORUGAI

PREPARATION TIME: 15 MIN
COOKING TIME: 15 MIN
MAKES: 2 JARS

INGREDIENTS

3 green (unripe) medium mangoes

½ tsp fenugreek seeds

¼ tsp asafoetida powder or ground asafoetida resin

2 tbsp coconut oil

½ tsp mustard seeds

1½ tsp salt

¼ tsp turmeric powder

1 tsp chilli powder

METHOD

1. Lightly dry-roast fenugreek seeds. Grind into a powder.
2. Chop green mangoes into small pieces (leaving skin on).
3. Heat coconut oil in a pan. Add mustard seeds and fry till they splutter.
4. Add chopped mango pieces, salt, fenugreek and asafoetida powder. Mix thoroughly. Cover and keep simmering.
5. After 5 minutes, uncover pan and stir mango mixture. Add turmeric and chilli powder. Mix well. Allow spices to seep in and remove pickle from the heat after about 2 more minutes.
6. When cool, store in sterilised airtight bottles or jars.

Mango Pickle / *A summer ritual of every family — the mango pickle preserves this fruit for use all year round. The sour flesh of green mango is balanced with salt and spice, as it languishes in a bath of coconut oil.*

THE ART OF PRESERVING FOODS

Umavati gently shares the valuable lessons of her *Ammama* (grandmother)
– which, even today, help her plan and prepare meals for her large and extended family.

Umavati's family were labourers on a farm, and her grandmother cooked in the farm
owner's house. She would often bring home leftover dishes and vegetables which she
would preserve, transforming the meal for the day into a delicacy that would last
for months, or a resource that could be called upon when she needed it.

Her *Ammama* showed her how to prepare yogurt from souring milk, fry eggplant
and *pavakkai* (bitter gourd), and how to dry fish for frying later on.

These dishes lasted for weeks if they were stored and preserved in the correct way.
Root vegetables and fish were wrapped in separate cloths and tied with string; jams
and yogurt were bottled and sealed. Umavati describes how her *Ammama* kept a rack
in the kitchen for preserving foods, away from the heat and steam of the open fire and
high up out of the reach of the roaming cat.

*These techniques for preserving food come
in handy nowadays when she knows she may
be out of work, out of money or out of time.
When she is, she looks to the high shelves in
her clay house to supply and sustain the family,
fondly remembering her Ammama's rituals.*

THAKKAALI YAAM

PREPARATION TIME: 30 MIN
COOKING TIME: 1 HR
MAKES: 1 JAR

INGREDIENTS

1kg tomatoes

1 star anise

2 cardamom pods

2 cloves

1 teaspoon black peppercorns

Juice of ½ an orange

Juice of ½ a lemon

Zest of ½ an orange

Zest of ½ a lemon

200g granulated sugar

METHOD

1. Fry off all the spices and when cool grind them until you get an even textured powder.
2. Chop tomatoes into small squares and put in a hot saucepan.
3. Add ground spices, lemon juice, lemon zest, orange juice, orange zest and sugar to the pan.
4. Keep stirring until sugar has dissolved completely then turn heat down and simmer for 40 minutes until a jam texture is achieved.
5. The jam can be stored in jars in the refrigerate for up to one month.

Tomato Jam / *A rich and mellow way to savour tomatoes, offering a sweet contrast to the tastes of spices and savoury dishes. It can accompany thosai, puttu, idli or rice.*

WE LIVE IN THE HOPE
THAT OUR CHILDREN
WILL BE ABLE TO
MAKE A LIVING
FOR THEMSELVES.

THENGAI-POO SAMBAL

Coconut Sambal / Fresh coconut and the sourness of tamarind are combined in a small pot, from which the fiery red colour and aroma of chilli emanates, beckoning to be eaten with the thosai, puttu, idli or other staple.

PREPARATION TIME: 10 MIN
COOKING TIME: 2 MIN
SERVINGS: 4

INGREDIENTS

½ cup grated coconut

1 tsp tamarind pulp (or lime juice)

6 dried red chillies

Salt (to taste)

4 tsp oil

1 onion, finely chopped

¼ tsp mustard seeds

¼ tsp black gram (ulunththu), split

1 sprig curry leaves

METHOD

1. Grind coconut, tamarind pulp, dried chillies and salt together.
2. Heat oil and fry the onion, mustard seeds, black gram and curry leaves.
3. Add onion mixture to coconut mixture and mix well. Serve as a side-dish.

PANANG-KILANGU THUVAIYAL

Palmyra Root Sambal /

Creamy white, fibrous, chewy the palmyra stays a while in the mouth, balanced softly with the moist delicateness of coconut. Together, they hold the flavour of chilli, releasing its heat at different rates.

PREPARATION TIME: 5 MIN
COOKING TIME: 45 MIN
SERVINGS: 4-6

INGREDIENTS

3 palmyra roots (frozen roots can be used)
4 cups water (or enough to cover roots while cooking)
1 green chilli, chopped
¼ cup grated coconut
Salt and pepper (to taste)

METHOD

1. Clean palmyra roots well to remove all soil and dirt. Wash thoroughly. Peel skin and wash again.
2. Boil roots in water until cooked. When cool, drain from water and roughly chop into small pieces.
3. Place palmyra root pieces, chilli and coconut in a mortar and pestle or a food processor. Cooks swear the *thuvaiyal* is best pounded in the traditional manner! Pound till well mixed.
4. Season with salt and pepper.
5. Serve as a side-dish with rice.

A *thuvaiyal* is a pounded vegetable dish, a great accompaniment to a rice meal. The simplicity of the dish belies its value in adding taste to a simple meal. An old adage goes *"You can eat rice with the fragrance of a thuvaiyal!"*

THE HUMBLE SOTHI

Vijaya's eyes glaze over as she fondly recalls her youth. Labouring on a farm, she worked all day picking green beans, collecting pumpkins and tending to the chickens. Her day's work would be rewarded with rice, beans, tomatoes, *murungakkai*, pumpkins and eggs, which she took home and eagerly transformed into a variety of dishes for her family of four.

In the 20 years since then, to escape the civil unrest, she has moved from village to village with her daughter Gayathri, her son-in-law and her granddaughter Anjali. She describes running between shelters to escape the shelling. Her voice grows quiet and heavy as she recalls when Anjali fell between some rocks and was injured. The family continued on the run for a few days filling their stomachs with rice, but they worried that Anjali was becoming weaker.

Then Gayathri left them in a desperate search for more food. Tears stream down Vijaya's face as she recalls the last time she saw her daughter.

Vijaya now looks after Anjali. She can hardly afford the regular supply of fresh and nutritious foods that Anjali needs to stay alert at school. Still, as Vijaya's animated hands return to her lap, she says that in the absence of green beans and pumpkins there are always *sothis* and *kulamboos* (a curry with a spoonable gravy, usually thick and spicy). Every day, each meal time, she takes great delight in watching little Anjali fastidiously lick her plate and fingers clean. It reminds her of the seriousness of her responsibility, and also brings her joy.

THAKKAALI SOTHI

Tomato and Coconut Milk Stew / *Cooked tomato is thickened with coconut milk and then again, luxuriously, with coconut cream. Its flavour is simple and piqued with the taste of lime. It is eagerly soaked up by the delicate bundles of idiappa.*

PREPARATION TIME: 5 MIN
COOKING TIME: 15 MIN
SERVINGS: 6

INGREDIENTS

2 tomatoes, quartered

3 cups water

3 or 4 green chillies, cut in half lengthways

1 onion, diced finely

¼ tsp fenugreek seeds

¼ tsp turmeric powder

½ cup coconut milk

½ tsp salt

½ cup coconut cream

1 tsp lime juice

METHOD

1. Boil tomatoes in water with green chillies, fenugreek seeds, turmeric powder, coconut milk and salt.
2. When tomatoes are soft, add coconut cream to the mixture.
3. Allow the mixture to come to boil again.
4. Remove from heat and add lime juice. Keep stirring to prevent curdling.
5. Remove and serve with idiappa.

> Traditionally *idiappa* are accompanied by, among other dishes, a coconut milk stew called *sothi*.

KOTHTHAMALLI RASAM

Coriander Broth / A hot, light and spicy broth, with clean, sharp flavours that breathe a fire into the belly, the chest and the tastebuds. Drink it on its own or let it smoothly engulf the plain rice it is paired with.

PREPARATION TIME: 5 MIN
COOKING TIME: 30 MIN
SERVINGS: 4

INGREDIENTS

3 tbsp coriander seeds

1 tsp cumin seeds

1 tsp black peppercorns

4 cloves garlic, roughly smashed

2 dried red chillies (or to taste)

3 cm piece dried ginger (ver kombu or chukku)

1 tomato or ½ can tinned tomatoes

2 tsp tamarind paste, dissolved in 1 tbsp water

Salt (to taste)

5 cups water

Handful coriander leaves, coarsely chopped

METHOD

1. Mix tamarind, water and salt.
2. Place coriander seeds, cumin seeds, peppercorns, red chillies and dried ginger in a mortar and pound it to a fine powder.
3. Roast powder in a saucepan until the aroma of the spices rises.
4. Add crushed garlic and sauté. Add tomatoes.
5. Add dissolved tamarind, water and salt to taste. Bring to boil and allow to simmer for at least 5 mins.
6. Remove. Garnish with chopped coriander.

MAINS

Arisi-maa Puttu	Muttai Rotti
Paal Puttu	Idiappam Buriyani
Odiyal Maa Puttu	Koththu Rotti
Maravalli Puttu	Godamba Rotti
Keerai Puttu	Murungakkai Kari
Appam	Kari-milaggai Kari
Idli	Meen Kari
Kundu Thosai	Paththiya Meen Kari
Kurakkan Rotti	Iraal Kari
Uppumaa	Koli Kari
Puli-saatham	Meen Varai
Idiappam	Suraa Varai
Thosai	Kanavaai Poriyal

DURING THE WAR IN VANNI, WE DIDN'T HAVE ACCESS TO A LOT OF KEY INGREDIENTS, SO THE KINDS OF FOOD WE COOKED DEPENDED ON WHAT WAS ALREADY BEING PRODUCED. FOR EXAMPLE WE WERE ABLE TO MAKE PUTTU USING RICE FLOUR (ARISI-MAA) BECAUSE RICE WAS BEING PRODUCED IN VANNI.

Steaming or roasting removes
stickiness of the flour. Steamed plain flour
can be purchased in Indian or Sri Lankan
grocery shops. To steam: place flour over
a cheesecloth, cover it with another piece
of cheesecloth and steam for 45 minutes.
Alternatively, use a pressure cooker
without the weight, so the steam escapes.
Once steamed, pass the flour through a sieve
and it is ready for use. For roasted plain flour,
place the flour in a wok or large pan
on medium heat and stir continuously for
10 minutes. It is then ready for use.

ARISI-MAA PUTTU

Steamed Rice Flour and Coconut / *Rice flour and coconut shreds are fused by steaming; and then crumbled by hand into fluffy morsels for eating with a curry.*

PREPARATION TIME: 10 MIN (+ STEAMING)
COOKING TIME: 20 MIN
SERVINGS: 3-4

Puttu is a popular breakfast dish. Traditionally a 'puttu kullal' made of bamboo was used to steam the dish, yielding a cylindrical log of puttu. Nowadays, stainless steel ones are more common and available in Indian and Sri Lankan grocery stores in all major cities. Before eating, puttu is broken by hand into smaller, fluffy morsels and mixed with a curry or even banana.

INGREDIENTS

2 cups white or red rice flour, steamed (see page 91)

1 tsp salt

2 cups boiling water (as required)

½ cup freshly grated coconut or desiccated coconut

REQUIRED

» Puttu steamer or other regular steamer
» Light cloth to line steamer

METHOD

1. In a large bowl, mix steamed flour and salt. Add boiling water slowly, mixing with a wooden spoon. When the mixture has cooled slightly, use hands to break down dough to create a grainy or pebbly texture. If too wet, add a little flour.

2. Add water to the pot of the steamer and heat the water to a boil. In the cylindrical body of the kullal (steamer), layer puttu mixture and coconut as follows: a handful of coconut, two handfuls of puttu dough, a handful of coconut, two handfuls puttu dough and so on, to about 1.5 cm from the top, the last layer being coconut. If using a regular steamer, line the base with a cloth and spread mixture and coconut evenly across the base.

3. Steam puttu till cooked. When cooked it should not be sticky to the touch.

4. Remove and push puttu out with the back of a wooden spoon into a bowl.

5. Repeat process till all dough is finished.

6. Serve warm with a sambal or curry.

PAAL PUTTU

Steamed Rice Flour and Coconut with
Milk / *A warm and luxurious breakfast of
puttu and coconut milk. The puttu softens in
the warm milk and, like porridge, nourishes
and satiates as it goes down.*

PREPARATION TIME: 10 MIN
(+ STEAMING)
COOKING TIME: 30 MIN
SERVINGS: 2

INGREDIENTS

1 cup rice flour, steamed (see page 91)

½ tsp salt

Boiling water (as required)

1 cup coconut milk

2 tbsp sugar

REQUIRED

» *Puttu* steamer or other regular steamer
» Light cloth to line steamer

METHOD

1. Place steamed flour and salt in a bowl.
2. Add boiling water very slowly, stirring flour
   constantly with a wooden spoon, to form a fairly stiff
   dough. Use hands to break down dough to create a
   grainy or pebbly texture. If too wet, add a little flour.
3. Add water to the pot of the steamer and heat the
   water to a boil.
4. Place the mixture in the cylindrical body of the kullal
   (steamer). If using a regular steamer, line the base
   with a cloth and spread mixture evenly across
   the base.
5. Steam the puttu till cooked. When cooked it should
   not be sticky to the touch. Remove and set aside.
6. Place coconut milk and sugar in a saucepan.
   Bring to boil.
7. Add the puttu to the saucepan, turn off heat
   and mix until milk is absorbed.
8. Serve warm.

PREPARATION TIME: 1 HR
COOKING TIME: 30 MIN
SERVINGS: 3-4

INGREDIENTS

250 g palmyra root flour (odiyal maa)

Water

¼ cup grated coconut

¼ cup water

½ tsp salt (or to taste)

REQUIRED

» Steamer
» Strainer
» Light cloth to line strainer and steamer

METHOD

1. Place palmyra root flour in a bowl.
2. Cover with water, to a few centimetres above flour level. Leave to soak for 15 minutes. This will remove much of the bitterness of stored flour.
3. Line a strainer with muslin cloth. Pour palmyra root flour and water through muslin cloth.
4. Lift cloth, gather the edges together and squeeze out all excess water. Repeat steps 1-4 as needed.
5. Place the damp flour in a bowl. Sprinkle salt and mix well by hand.
6. Add grated coconut and mix.
7. Add water to the pot of the steamer and heat the water to a boil.
8. Line steamer with a thin cloth. Make small balls of the mix and place these on the steamer. Steam for a few minutes.
9. Remove from steamer and serve warm with a coconut chutney, coriander leaf chutney or a curry.

ODIYAL MAA PUTTU

Steamed Palmyra Root Flour and Coconut / *The palmyra and coconut, whose trees dominate Sri Lanka's landscape and support the life of its people, come together in this staple, a variant on the traditional puttu.*

Steamed Cassava and Coconut / *Freshly steamed, the fibres of the cassava expand with warm air and moisture, exuding puffs of steam when broken. Gratings of coconut, moist and milky, balance the taste and interrupt the fibrous texture.*

MARAVALLI PUTTU

PREPARATION TIME: 30 MIN (+ DRYING)
COOKING TIME: 20 MIN
SERVINGS: 2-3

INGREDIENTS

250 g cassava, peeled, washed and cut into small pieces (frozen cassava can be used)

½ tsp salt

¼ cup freshly grated coconut

Boiling water (as required)

REQUIRED

» Puttu steamer or a regular steamer
» Light cloth to line steamer

METHOD

1. Place cassava pieces (fresh or frozen) on a tray and allow to dry thoroughly (inside or outside). When completely dry and slightly shrivelled, pound finely in a mortar or grind using a food processor.
2. Spread pounded cassava on a tray, and remove any large, fibrous bits.
3. Place ground cassava in a bowl with salt. Add boiling water, a little at a time and mix with a wooden spoon until dough is grainy.
4. Add grated coconut and mix by hand.
5. Add salt to taste.
6. Add water to the pot of the steamer and heat the water to a boil.
7. Place mixture in the cylindrical body of the *kullal* (steamer). If using a regular steamer, line the base with a cloth and spread mixture evenly across the base.
8. Steam puttu till cooked. When cooked it should not be sticky to the touch.
9. Remove from steamer and serve warm.

KEERAI PUTTU

Steamed Spinach and Coconut /
Green streaks of spinach and onion bits transform the traditional puttu into a dish that can be eaten on its own. Plain flour adds to its robustness.

PREPARATION TIME: 30 MIN (+ STEAMING)
COOKING TIME: 30 MIN
SERVINGS: 4

INGREDIENTS

4 cups plain flour, steamed (see page 91)

1 tsp salt

Boiling water (as required)

1½ cups spinach, chopped finely

½ cup coconut, freshly grated

2 green chillies, chopped finely

2 medium red onions, chopped finely (optional, for a savoury taste)

REQUIRED

» Puttu steamer or a regular steamer
» Light cloth to line steamer

METHOD

1. Mix steamed flour and salt in a bowl. Add the boiling water slowly and stir with a wooden spoon till it forms a stiff dough. Work the dough with your hands to form a grainy, pebbly texture. If the dough becomes too wet, add a little more flour.

2. Add the spinach, coconut, green chillies and onions (if using). Mix well.

3. Add water to the pot of the steamer and heat the water to a boil.

4. Place mixture in the cylindrical body of the *kullal* (steamer). If using a regular steamer, line the base with a cloth and spread mixture evenly across the base.

5. Steam puttu till cooked. When cooked it should not be sticky to the touch.

6. Remove from steamer and serve warm with a chutney or curry.

NOTHING BEATS HOMEMADE

The thought of *appam* makes Anupama beam with delight. Her mind returns to her teenage days when, after school, she helped her mother grind rice flour on the *ammi* (grinding stone). They would mix a large bowl of the fine flour with *toddy* (a coconut-based alcohol), work it intensively, and then leave it to ferment overnight. In the morning her mother would stir freshly made coconut milk into the fluffy flour mixture. She would then pour the batter into shiny steel dishes that were heated on the open fire. The crispy *appams* took the shape of the bowl. Anupama would pour extra coconut milk over her *appam* while her mother cracked an egg on her brother's.

Anupama clearly revels in describing each ingredient: the coconut, the rice and ghee, all fresh from their garden or farm, and transformed in the kitchen by mother and daughter.

Anupama has not made *appam* in a long time, even though it is a simple staple. She does not have fresh enough ingredients, or the right utensils at home. These days there are instant mixtures, but she worries that her children already eat enough packaged and preserved foods.

Anupama often walks down Kandy Road past the stalls that serve up appam, but she does not stop. She doesn't crave these appams. She keeps walking, refusing to have memories of her mother's fresh, handmade crispy appams tarnished by with these imposters made from instant mixtures. Instead, she conjures up her appam, with its aroma, its softness and its delicate taste made from the freshest ingredients.

APPAM

Hoppers / *Warm, fluffy appams have thick, soft middles that radiate out to a delicate, crispy edge. They are eaten sweet with thick coconut milk and sugar in the centre, or with a curry and coconut or onion sambal. Sometimes the appam has an egg firmly planted at its centre.*

PREPARATION TIME: 15 MIN
(+ FERMENTING)
COOKING TIME: 20 MIN
MAKES: 8

INGREDIENTS

2 cups rice flour (to vary texture a handful 'broken rice' or ¼ cup plain flour can be substituted)

1 tsp sugar

Pinch of baking powder

½ tsp salt

1½ cups coconut milk (more if necessary)

Oil to grease the appams pans

Eggs (for egg appams)

REQUIRED

» Appams pan (appa chatti)

METHOD

1. In a bowl, mix rice flour (with broken rice flour and plain flour if using), sugar, baking powder, salt and coconut milk. Mix it thoroughly to remove lumps; it should run easily from your fingertips.
2. Cover and set aside in a warm place to ferment for 12-18 hours.
3. Mix again. Add more coconut milk if necessary, and mix.
4. Grease appams pan (not necessary for non-stick pans) and place over medium heat. When pan is hot, pour a spoonful of mixture into the centre, lift pan and swirl batter around to thinly coat the sides of the pan. Cover and cook.
5. When the edges turn crisp and lace-like, slide the appams out of the pan.

For a sweet appams, pour a tablespoon of thick coconut milk into the centre, and sprinkle with sugar or brown sugar when almost cooked.

For an egg appams, break an egg into the centre of the appams as soon as it is poured in. Cover and cook. Slide out when done.

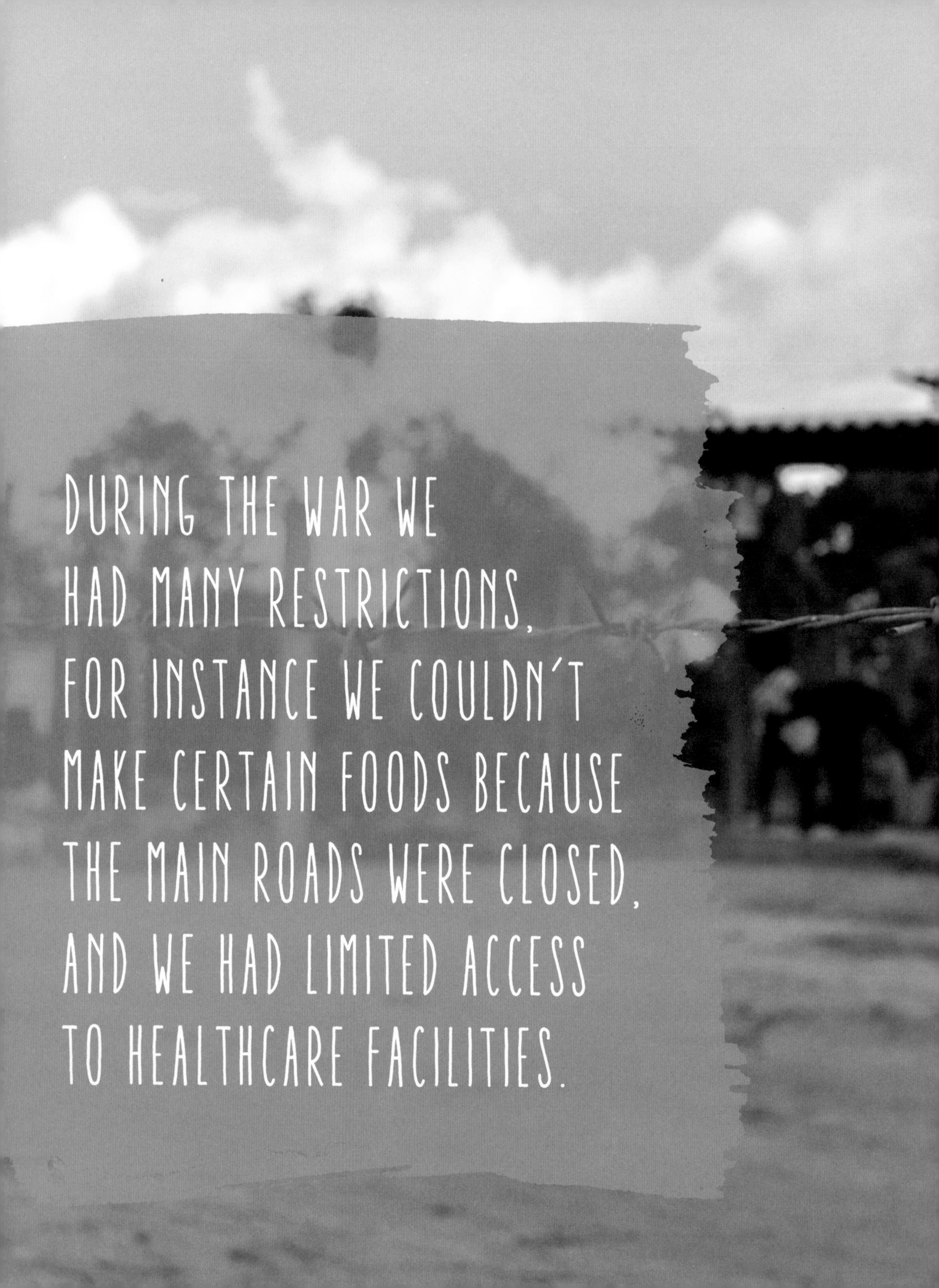

DURING THE WAR WE
HAD MANY RESTRICTIONS,
FOR INSTANCE WE COULDN'T
MAKE CERTAIN FOODS BECAUSE
THE MAIN ROADS WERE CLOSED,
AND WE HAD LIMITED ACCESS
TO HEALTHCARE FACILITIES.

IDLI

Steamed Rice Cakes / *A light, fluffy staple that makes regular appearances at breakfast time, its steam heralding a delicious trio in combination with sambar and coconut chutney.*

PREPARATION TIME: 15 MIN
(+ SOAKING, FERMENTATION)
COOKING TIME: 20 MIN
SERVINGS: 6

INGREDIENTS

1 cup black gram (ulunththu), skinless and split, soaked overnight

2 cups idli rice or parboiled rice, soaked overnight

1 tsp salt

Oil sesame (gingelly) or coconut

REQUIRED

» Idli steamer

METHOD

1. Drain rice and black gram and grind both grains separately to a fine consistency. The ground rice should be like thick pancake batter, but still grainy. The ground black gram should be thicker, almost doughy.

2. Mix ground black gram and ground rice in a large bowl, cover with a cloth and leave to ferment overnight.

3. Add salt and mix well.

4. Grease the idli moulds with oil and pour a spoonful of batter in each mould and steam until it is cooked (the idlis should not be sticky to the touch or leave any residue when pierced with a fork/skewer).

5. Serve warm with coconut chutney and sambar.

Thosai Balls / *Thosai, traditionally flat and thin, is squeezed into the shape of round dumplings and cooked over a flame in a kuli paniyaaram pan. The women have crafted a staple with the most basic of ingredients to be eaten with coconut chutneys or curries. It is also called kuli thosai or kuli paniyaaram.*

KUNDU THOSAI

PREPARATION TIME: 45 MIN
(+ FERMENTATION)
COOKING TIME: 10-15 MIN
MAKES: 40-45

INGREDIENTS

1 cup black gram (ulunththu), skinless, split, soaked for at least 6 hours

½ cup plain flour, steamed (see page 91)

½ cup plain flour, unsteamed

½ tsp baking soda (appa soda)

½ tsp salt

¼ cup water

Sesame (gingelly) oil

Chopped onions and green chillies, and grated carrot (optional, for a savoury snack)

REQUIRED

» Kuli paniyaaram mould or a baking tray with circular depressions

METHOD

1. Drain soaked black gram. Grind finely using a grinder or food processor.
2. In a bowl, mix ground black gram, plain flour (both steamed and raw), baking soda and salt. Mix well to remove lumps. Add water and mix into a smooth batter.
3. Set aside batter to ferment for 6-8 hours. Add onions, chillies and carrot (if using).
4. Grease moulds and fill each with a spoonful of batter.
5. Cook over medium heat until the edges are dry and turn brown. Using a skewer or a fork, turn the kundu *thosai* to cook on the other side.
6. Remove from moulds when cooked. Serve warm with chutney or a curry.

KURAKKAN ROTTI

Millet (Raagi) Rotti / *Kurakkan, with its deep red-purple hue, is filled with protein and has a rich, nutty flavour. Ground into a flour, its little black grains dot the rotti, and with the light softness of coconut, provide a nourishing staple. The rotti has a slightly tougher texture than a pancake and is traditionally paired with seeni sambal, a coconut-based dry side-dish.*

PREPARATION TIME: 15 MIN
COOKING TIME: 5 MIN
MAKES: 15-20

INGREDIENTS

1 cup kurakkan flour

½ cup plain flour (optional – kurakkan flour alone can be used, but the rotti becomes very brittle – adding up to ½ cup plain flour softens the rotti)

1 cup grated coconut

½ tsp salt

½ cup brown sugar

Water (as required)

Coconut or other vegetable oil

METHOD

1. Place all dry ingredients in a bowl.
2. Add water gradually until dough becomes stiff. Grease hands with oil to make it easier to knead. Knead dough well. Take a handful of dough and make into small balls, 3-4 cm in diameter.
3. Flatten each ball on a greased banana leaf or other non-stick surface, till it is like a pancake, 2-3 mm in thickness.
4. Heat a griddle or pan and smear with oil. Cook rotti on one side and flip over to cook other side. Remove from griddle when done.
5. Serve warm.

Kurakkan belongs to the 'millet' group of cereals and in English is known as 'finger millet', or '*raagi*' in India. Millet is one of the oldest foods known to humans. "*So much nutrition,*" says a mother. "*I kept us alive through making kurakkan puttu and kurakkan rotti.*"

In the days before the war we made our own
rice flour, grinding the rice ourselves.

Now we rely on packaged foods and flours. We do not have the facilities to
make the foods we used to make. Now it is convenient but not as tasty.

We had our own cows and fresh milk.
Vegetables were in vast supply.
Green mangoes and green bananas abounded.
Rice was so cheap.

Fresh fruits are expensive. Now we have processed foods, sodas,
biscuits, Milo and juice.

In those days children didn't get as sick.
We used a lot of herbal medicine like curry leaves.

Kurakkan maa is low in stock. There is no *saamai rice* for diabetic people.
Now we are just given medicines.

Ghee was widely available. Honey too.
And sherbet was something we enjoyed.

Now there is no ghee. Or sherbet.
We look at shops making it and like food critics we review their concoctions.

Honey, but honey, yes we can still get hold of this.

Stir-fried Semolina with Vegetables / *Soft semolina, with smatterings of colour — red chilli, green beans, carrots, dark mustard seeds, and its variegated textures, is a feast for all the senses.*

UPPUMAA

PREPARATION TIME: 20 MIN
COOKING TIME: 45 MIN
SERVINGS: 4

INGREDIENTS

1¼ cups semolina (the coarser the better)

1 tbsp coconut, sesame (gingelly) oil or ghee

2 dried red chillies, broken into pieces

1 tsp mustard seeds

7-8 curry leaves

½ medium onion, chopped

4 green chillies, chopped roughly

6 beans, cut into small pieces

1 carrot, coarsely grated

¼ cabbage, chopped finely

1 leek, white part only, chopped finely

1 cup water

½ cup milk

Salt (to taste)

METHOD

1. Dry-roast semolina in a pan for 10 minutes.
2. In another pan, heat oil or ghee over medium heat. Add red chillies and mustard seeds.
3. When mustard seeds splutter, add chopped onion, green chillies and curry leaves. Sauté until onions are golden-brown.
4. Add beans, carrot, cabbage and leek and cook till tender.
5. Add water and salt and bring to boil.
6. Reduce heat and slowly add semolina, stirring constantly to avoid lumps.
7. Continue stirring until all water is absorbed and uppumaa is cooked.
8. Remove from heat and serve warm.

PULI-SAATHAM

Tamarind Rice / *An ode to the endless possibilities of rice, this preparation uses seeds, herbs and lentils to create a dish that can satiate on its own.*

PREPARATION TIME: 10 MIN
COOKING TIME: 30 MIN
SERVINGS: 2-3

INGREDIENTS

1 cup samba rice (or other long-grain rice eg, basmati)

2 tbsp sesame (gingelly) oil

1 large brown onion or 8 small rose onions, sliced finely

4 dried red chillies, broken into pieces

½ tsp mustard seeds

½ tsp fennel seeds

1 tbsp black gram (ulunththu), skinless

2 tsp chilli powder

½ tsp turmeric powder

½ tsp fenugreek powder

1 sprig curry leaves

2 tbsp thick tamarind pulp

½ tsp asafoetida powder, dissolved in 2 tbsp warm water

Salt (to taste)

METHOD

1. Cook rice using preferred method. When cooked, fork through to separate grains and set aside to cool.
2. Place medium-sized frying pan over medium heat and pour in gingelly oil.
3. When oil is hot, add sliced onions and fry till translucent.
4. Add mustard seeds and fennel seeds. Cook till they splutter. Add black gram.
5. Add chilli powder, turmeric powder, fenugreek powder, broken dried chilli pieces and curry leaves.
6. As fragrance rises, add tamarind pulp and asafoetida water.
7. Bring to boil, then remove from heat.
8. Add cooked rice to pan and stir thoroughly until rice is well coated in the spice mixture and turns a warm golden-brown.
9. Serve warm or cold.

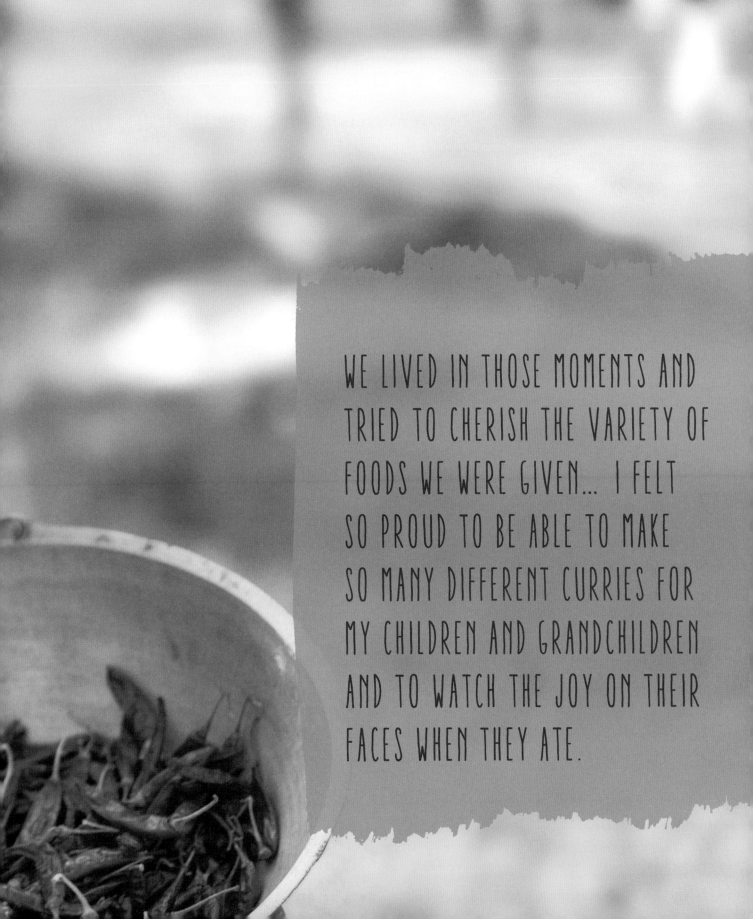

WE LIVED IN THOSE MOMENTS AND TRIED TO CHERISH THE VARIETY OF FOODS WE WERE GIVEN... I FELT SO PROUD TO BE ABLE TO MAKE SO MANY DIFFERENT CURRIES FOR MY CHILDREN AND GRANDCHILDREN AND TO WATCH THE JOY ON THEIR FACES WHEN THEY ATE.

IDIAPPAM

String Hoppers / *Idiappam is a quintessentially Sri Lankan breakfast dish. To form the stringy, lace-like creations, you need an idiappam press. Idiappam is traditionally paired with a curry like sothi (page 83), coconut sambal or an omelette.*

PREPARATION TIME: 10 MIN
COOKING TIME: 15 MIN
MAKES: 20-30

INGREDIENTS
2 cups white or red rice flour, dry-roasted

½ tsp salt

Boiling water (as required)

REQUIRED
» Idiappam press (ural)
» Idiappa steamer (avikrer chatti) or alternative steamer

METHOD
1. Mix flour and salt in a bowl. Add enough boiling water to form a dry-ish dough, and stir with a wooden spoon to combine. The dough should not be sticky to the touch.
2. Using an idiappam ural, form the idiappa on a steamer tray.
3. When you have made enough idiappa to cover the tray, steam them till they are not sticky to the touch.
4. Keep cooked idiappa warm in oven on a low setting until all are cooked. Serve with sothi or dhal, and coconut sambal.

THOSAI

Savoury Rice Pancakes /

This is a popular breakfast or dinner dish in Sri Lanka. These fermented pancakes are called 'dosa' in India, with many variants in fillings.

PREPARATION TIME: 20 MIN
(+ SOAKING, FERMENTATION)
COOKING TIME: 20 MIN
SERVINGS: 3-4

INGREDIENTS

½ cup idli or parboiled rice

½ cup long-grain rice

1 cup black gram (ulunththu), split and skinless

1 tsp fenugreek seeds

1 tsp salt

METHOD

1. Mix both types of rice. Wash well and cover with water in a bowl and allow to soak for at least 4 hours. Wash and soak black gram and fenugreek seeds together for 4 hours.
2. Drain and grind soaked rice in a wet grinder or food processor until very fine and smooth. Add water if necessary to thin batter to a pouring consistency.
3. Repeat Step 2 with black gram and fenugreek seeds.
4. Mix both ground batters in a large bowl. Add salt.
5. Cover and set aside to ferment for 6-8 hours in a warm place.
6. When ready to make thosai, mix batter well. If too thick, add a little water and mix.
7. Grease a flat pan or pancake griddle.
8. Spoon a ladle of batter onto the pan and smooth into a circle with the back of the ladle (move it from the centre in a clockwise direction to spread the batter into a circle). Place a smear of ghee or sesame (gingelly) oil on thosai if desired.
9. When the bottom turns golden, and bubbles appear in the thosai, remove.
10. Keep thosai warm and continue making pancakes until the batter is used up. Serve warm with a vegetable side, coconut chutney and/or sambar.

MUTTAI ROTTI

Sweet Egg and Rice Pancake /

With rice for texture, dhal for protein, coconut milk to soften, jaggery to sweeten and eggs to bind, this is a nutritious and compact breakfast. It is often given to girls through puberty, to expectant mothers or as a general 'pick-me-up'. Though called a rotti, it is more like a pancake.

PREPARATION TIME: 10 MIN
COOKING TIME: 20-30 MIN
MAKES: 8 (10 CM DIAMETER)

INGREDIENTS

1 cup rice flour

½ cup black gram flour (ulunththa maa)

1 cup coconut milk

1 cup jaggery, pounded finely

1 egg, beaten well

½ tsp salt (or to taste)

METHOD

1. Mix all ingredients until there are no lumps.
2. Grease a griddle or a pan with a flat bottom.
3. Using a ladle, spoon some mix onto the pan to form *rotti*, as you would make pancakes or thosai. Cook on both sides and remove. Repeat until mix is finished.
4. Serve warm with a chutney or curry.

IDIAPPAM BURIYANI

String Hopper Biryani /

Soft, stringy idiappa coated in the moist, thick flavours of biryani is a lighter alternative to the traditional rice dish. This recipe makes use of the string hoppers left over from breakfast, and any vermicelli-like noodles for example, of rice or green gram beans, can be substituted.

PREPARATION TIME: 20 MIN
COOKING TIME: 45 MIN
SERVINGS: 4

INGREDIENTS

16 fresh idiappam (string hoppers, red or white rice) (see page 123)

4 small–medium potatoes, cut into small cubes

2 tsp salt

2 tsp chilli powder

2 eggplants, cut into small cubes

Oil for deep-frying

20 green beans, cut into small pieces

2 carrots, grated coarsely

¼ green cabbage (small), chopped finely

2 leeks, white part only, chopped finely

2 eggs, beaten lightly with salt and chilli powder (to taste)

2 onions, chopped

6 green chillies, sliced

2 sprigs fresh curry leaves

METHOD

1. Marinate cubed potatoes with 1 teaspoon salt and 1 teaspoon chilli powder. Set aside for a few minutes.
2. Marinate eggplant with 1 teaspoon salt and 1 teaspoon chilli powder. Set aside for a few minutes.
3. Heat oil over medium-high heat. Deep-fry the potatoes. Drain onto absorbent paper.
4. Deep-fry the eggplant. Drain and keep with fried potatoes.
5. Break up string hoppers into small pieces.
6. Heat a little oil in a pan, add onions, green chillies and curry leaves and sauté until onions are golden-brown.
7. Add beaten eggs and fry till eggs are cooked. Break resulting omelette into pieces.
8. Add beans, carrot, cabbage and leek, and cook till tender.
9. Add string hoppers, fried potatoes and fried eggplant and mix thoroughly.
10. Remove from heat and serve warm.

KUMAR AND HIS KOTHTHU

Smiling coyly, Kamaleshwari admits that she barely knew how to cook when she got married. She was orphaned as a young girl and was moved frequently to different homes and orphanages around the Vavuniya district.

She beams as she describes the dishes she learned to make from Kumar, her husband. He also lost his mother but learned how to make food from his aunts. Kamaleshwari says with great pride that her husband knew all the dishes, from main meals and sweets to *palaharams* prepared on special occasions.

After Kumar was paralysed from his torso down, Kamaleshwari became the main breadwinner in the house. Her cheeks blush with pride as she speaks of her husband. Kumar knew Kamaleshwari enjoyed eating out, especially *koththu rotti*. But he refused to buy it from the street stalls because he knew how to prepare it at home. Kamaleshwari excitedly describes how her husband kneaded and chopped the *rotti*, and then stirred it into the crackling frying pan containing her favourite mix of eggs, carrots, cabbage, leeks, beans and chicken. She reiterated that Kumar was a very thoughtful man, and he wrapped and served the chicken *koththu* in newspaper, just like in the takeaway stalls.

Sadness crosses Kamaleshwari's face as she says that she is now alone: Kumar passed away a year ago from a kidney infection. But she says that she is very fortunate that she had such a wonderful husband. Often as she walks down the street at dusk, she thinks of Kumar. She stops at a stall to order some *koththu* and, remembering him, smiles at his insistence on cooking at home.

Chopped Rotti Stir-fry / *Cooked, or rather, performed on the streets after dusk, koththu is so commonly eaten by all communities that it passes as a Sri Lankan specialty. It is said to have come from the Muslims of the north-east. The rhythmic clanging of metal against metal as the vegetables, egg and left-over curry are chopped (koththu), makes the mouth water and heart patter in anticipation of a plateful.*

KOTHTHU ROTTI

PREPARATION TIME: 30 MIN
COOKING TIME: 15 MIN
SERVINGS: 4

INGREDIENTS

3-4 godamba rottis

1 tbsp vegetable oil

1 onion, chopped

6 small (or 2-3 large) green chillies, sliced thinly

1 sprig curry leaves

2 eggs, beaten with salt and chilli powder (to taste)

10 green beans, cut into small pieces

1 carrot, grated coarsely

⅛ cabbage, chopped finely

1 leek, white part only, chopped finely

1 cup leftover vegetarian or meat curry (see page 156)

METHOD

1. Roughly chop *rottis* into small pieces.
2. Heat oil in a wok. Add onions, green chillies and curry leaves and sauté until onions are golden-brown.
3. Add beaten eggs and fry till cooked. Break up cooked eggs into pieces in the pot with a spatula.
4. Add beans, carrot, cabbage and leek and cook till tender.
5. Add chopped *rottis* and mix thoroughly.
6. Add curry and mix well.
7. Remove from heat and serve.

Godamba rottis, a flat bread of plain flour, are available in most Sri Lankan grocery stores. In their absence Indian *parathas* or Malaysian *rotti chanai* may be used. To make your own see the recipe for *godamba rotti* on page 136. Rottis can be prepared several hours ahead and stored for use later.

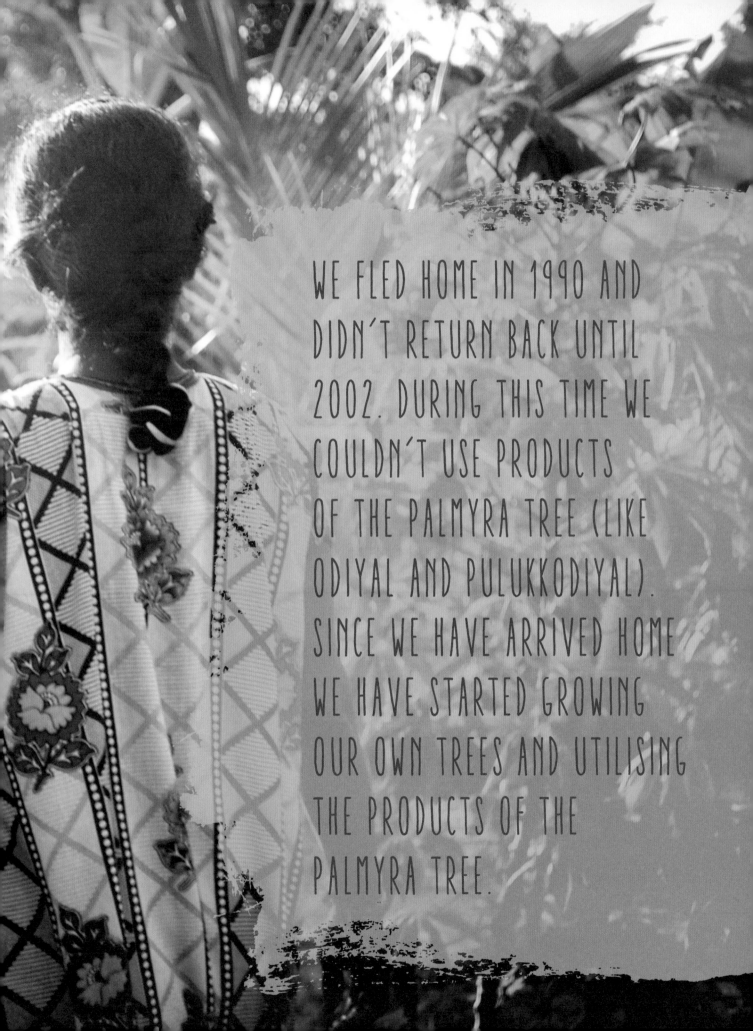

WE FLED HOME IN 1990 AND DIDN'T RETURN BACK UNTIL 2002. DURING THIS TIME WE COULDN'T USE PRODUCTS OF THE PALMYRA TREE (LIKE ODIYAL AND PULUKKODIYAL). SINCE WE HAVE ARRIVED HOME WE HAVE STARTED GROWING OUR OWN TREES AND UTILISING THE PRODUCTS OF THE PALMYRA TREE.

GODAMBA ROTTI

Plain Rotti

PREPARATION TIME: 20 MIN
(+ OVERNIGHT)
COOKING TIME: 20 MIN
MAKES: 6-8

INGREDIENTS

250 g self-raising flour

Pinch of salt

Water (as required)

1 cup coconut or vegetable oil

METHOD

1. Place flour and salt in a bowl.
2. Add water slowly and knead to make smooth dough. The dough should not be sticky. Once kneaded, form little balls with dough.
3. Pour oil into a flat-bottomed tray. Coat each ball with the oil and leave on the tray. Cover and leave for a few hours, at minimum, or overnight.
4. When ready to make *rottis*, take balls of dough and flatten each into a 3-4 cm circle.
5. Heat frying pan. Cook each rotti separately, drizzling oil onto pan to prevent *rottis* from sticking. Turn over after about 30 seconds and cook on other side. Once cooked through, place *rottis* onto plate. Use as desired, either warm or at room temperature.

"Meat for vegetarians, my mother used to say," says young Prema as she cradles her newborn and rocks him gently.

Murungakkai is one of the most popular vegetables prepared for women during and after pregnancy. Prema was given drumstick curry as often as her mother could get hold of it in the last month of her pregnancy. "*My mother said it would help with the delivery of the baby – though I don't know how!*" After the birth, drumstick curry with very young green *brinjals* (eggplant) was part of her *paththiyam* (confinement) diet. The vegetables help to heal wounds and ease the discomfort of childbirth in the days immediately after. The local midwife adds later: "*It stops the new mother from feeling depressed after childbirth.*" An antidote for post-natal depression too, it seems.

The leaves of the tree are even more nutritious than the fruit, being richer in calcium than milk and containing nearly all the amino acids required by the human body. A handful of leaves thrown into porridges, vegetables and stews are a rich source of Vitamins A, B, C and E and the minerals potassium, calcium and iron.

Drumstick curry and drumstick leaf *vadaham* (fritter) are regular features at the midday meal. It often follows the weekly oil bath, where the body is massaged with *gingelly* oil, which is left on for a couple of hours, before being washed away in a hot shower. The curry restores energy and strengthens the body against chills.

The *murungakkai* tree is revered as a miracle tree for its medicinal, nutritional and purifying properties. The finger-like green pods house rich nourishment, healing life during its most fragile stages. It is enjoyed greatly also because it demands a conscious attention to hold the sticks and chew out the goodness – well chewed fibres on the plate telling of how delicious the food was, or perhaps how hungry the eater.

PREPARATION TIME: 10 MIN
COOKING TIME: 20 MIN
SERVES: 4-6

INGREDIENTS

400 g or 4 long drumsticks (murungakkai)
4 tbsp oil
1 tsp fenugreek seeds
10 small onions (or 1 large onion), chopped
10 cloves garlic, chopped finely
3 green chillies, slit lengthways
4 tsp curry powder
1 tsp salt
1½ cups water
1 cup coconut milk
1 tsp tamarind pulp (or ½ tsp tamarind paste)
1 sprig curry leaves

METHOD

1. Scrape outside of drumsticks lengthways to remove excess fibrous covering. Cut them into 7 cm pieces and cut open lengthways down the middle.
2. Heat oil in a saucepan. Add fenugreek seeds and fry till golden-brown.
3. Add onions, garlic and green chillies. Fry till onions are golden-brown.
4. Add drumsticks to fried ingredients.
5. Add curry powder, salt and water.
6. Cover and cook till drumsticks are tender.
7. Add coconut milk and tamarind pulp or paste. Stir mixture gently.
8. Simmer for about 3 minutes.
9. Add curry leaves and remove from heat.
10. Serve warm with rice.

Drumstick Curry / *Short, fibrous sticks lie in a delicious gravy. Thick ones, thin ones. There is a tussle for who gets the biggest serve of drumsticks over their rice. First the curry is licked off, then the pulpy insides are scraped and finally the drumsticks are chewed through, lying like tangled straw on the empty plate.*

MURUNGAKKAI KARI

KARI-MILAGGAI KARI

PREPARATION TIME: 15 MIN
COOKING TIME: 30 MIN
SERVINGS: 4

Hot Chilli Curry / *Glossy, green chillies float in an earthy green stew, creamed with the taste of coconut and the thickness of potatoes.*

INGREDIENTS

6 large green chillies (long chillies, can be hot or mild)

1 medium potato, cubed (other vegetables like green peas, eggplant or okra can be added for variety)

10 small rose onions (or 1 medium red onion), chopped finely

1 tbsp oil

¼ tsp fennel seeds

¼ tsp fenugreek seeds

5 or 6 curry leaves

1 cup coconut milk (or milk from ½ coconut)

½ tsp curry powder

¼ tsp salt

METHOD

1. Slit chillies in half lengthways and remove seeds.
2. Heat oil. Sauté fennel seeds, fenugreek seeds and curry leaves.
3. Add chopped onions.
4. Add cubed potato and green chillies. Toss together.
5. Add curry powder and coconut milk. Add salt to taste. Mix well.
6. Lower heat and allow to cook for a few minutes.
7. Bring to boil, mix again and cook for a further two minutes. If consistency becomes too thick before potato is cooked through, add ¼ cup water.
8. Remove from heat and serve with rice.

THE MERMAID AND THE FISHERMAN

Selvarani comes from the port town of Trincomalee, or 'Trinco', where fish is in constant supply. As a child, she lived comfortably, with an abundance of food, at least before her father was killed. After his death she and her mother struggled, and her mother took up sewing to make ends meet. Despite the hardships, her mother usually prepared a fish curry or fried fish and rice. This was their staple.

Selvarani describes the fish curry, the only dish she learned to make from her mother. She places an imaginary fish on her lap and cleans its scales carefully, preserving as much flesh as possible. Every part of the fish is used: the head, the gills, the eyes and bones add flavour and texture to the curry. She keeps going, slicing thick chunks of fish in the air. She uses a clay pot to make her curry, with chopped onions, chillies, turmeric, tamarind and garlic. When she can get hold of cumin and fenugreek seeds she adds these to the boiling pot. She then adds milk and simmers the fish. The cow's milk is a substitute for the more flavoursome coconut milk she used to use. The curry made with a whole fish can last her family a day or two.

Happily, a husband is part of Selvarani's story; they married in 2011, after the war – after she lost a leg to a land mine. Her husband is from Jaffna and learned to cook from his mother. He helps her make the dough for *idiappam* and *puttu*. She says he stirs the dough well and knows how to make them soft and tidily. She, on the other hand, makes a mess.

She is still happily preparing and eating fish curry – but now it's with her husband.

WE STILL COOK AT HOME USING A FIREWOOD STOVE (VIRAGU ADUPPU) BECAUSE THE FOOD TASTES BETTER. THIS MAY CHANGE IN THE FUTURE. IN FACT LOTS OF PEOPLE HAVE ALREADY STOPPED USING WOOD FIRE STOVES, BUT WE MUST ENCOURAGE THEM TO CONTINUE USING IT BECAUSE FOOD COOKED THIS WAY TASTES BETTER AND IS HEALTHIER.

MEEN KARI

Fish Curry / *Thick pieces of fish swimming in an aromatic, milky curry, whose taste varies at the hand of each cook. Each time however, as it is spooned over puttu, idiappa or rice it yields a warm feeling of satiation. Fish curry is traditionally prepared in a clay pot (mann chatti), drawing in an earthy, full flavour.*

PREPARATION TIME: 15 MIN
COOKING TIME: 30 MIN
SERVINGS: 5-6

INGREDIENTS

1 kg any firm fish, cut into thick slices

1 onion, chopped

2 green chillies, slit lengthways and cut into pieces

½ tsp turmeric powder

1 tsp thick tamarind pulp mixed in 1 tbsp water

4 tsp curry powder

½ tsp salt (or to taste)

8 cloves garlic, peeled and crushed roughly

2 cups water

¼ tsp cumin seed powder

¼ tsp ground pepper

½ cup coconut milk

1½ tsp fenugreek seeds

1 sprig curry leaves

METHOD

1. Place chopped onions, green chillies, turmeric powder, tamarind water, curry powder, salt, garlic and water in a saucepan. Bring to boil.
2. Add fish slices.
3. Add cumin seed powder and ground pepper. Add fenugreek seeds.
4. Add coconut milk and curry leaves. Bring to boil. Lower heat and stir curry gently. Simmer for about 2 minutes.
5. Remove from heat and serve.

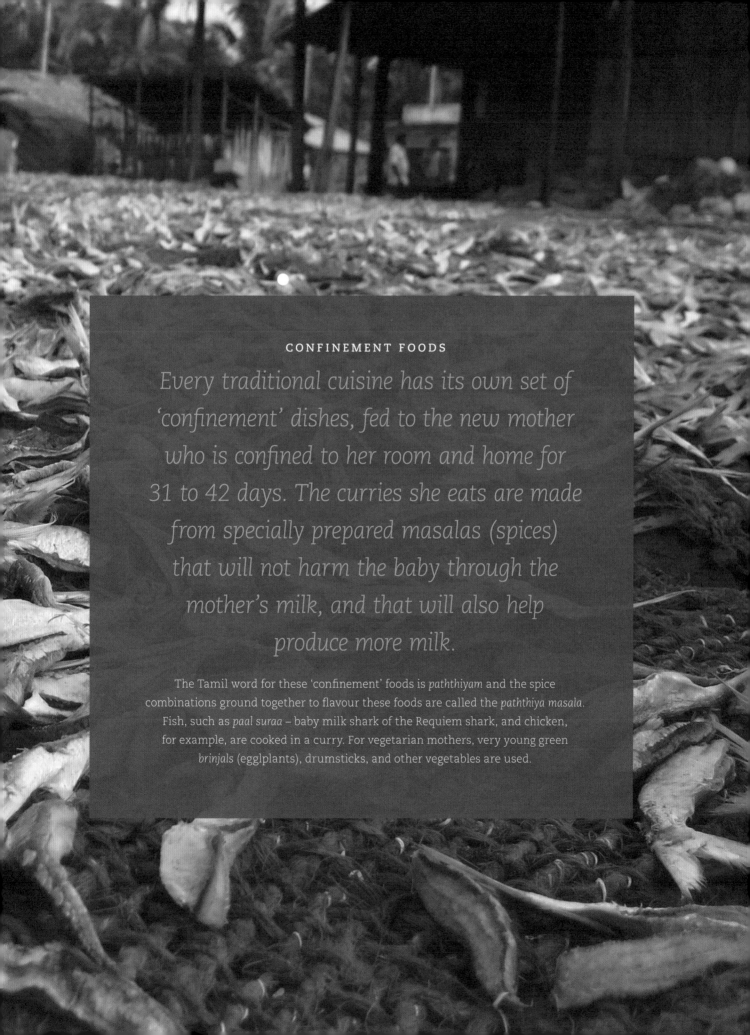

CONFINEMENT FOODS

Every traditional cuisine has its own set of 'confinement' dishes, fed to the new mother who is confined to her room and home for 31 to 42 days. The curries she eats are made from specially prepared masalas (spices) that will not harm the baby through the mother's milk, and that will also help produce more milk.

The Tamil word for these 'confinement' foods is *paththiyam* and the spice combinations ground together to flavour these foods are called the *paththiya masala*. Fish, such as *paal suraa* – baby milk shark of the Requiem shark, and chicken, for example, are cooked in a curry. For vegetarian mothers, very young green *brinjals* (egglplants), drumsticks, and other vegetables are used.

PATHTHIYA MEEN KARI

Confinement Fish Curry /

Traditionally prepared for women who have just given birth, this clear broth is a smooth blend of spices with a touch of tamarind.

PREPARATION TIME: 20 MIN
COOKING TIME: 35 MIN
SERVINGS: 4-5

INGREDIENTS

For the paste:

8 tsp coriander seeds

2 tsp cumin seeds

2 tsp peppercorns

2 dried red chillies

8 tbsp grated coconut (or 8 tbsp coconut milk)

For the curry:

3 cups water

800 g firm fish pieces, traditionally milk shark (paal suraa)

10 small rose onions or shallots (or 3 medium onions)

1 tsp fenugreek seeds

10 cloves garlic, pounded

1 tsp turmeric powder

Salt (to taste)

2 sprigs curry leaves

Tamarind (2 tsp dried or 1 tsp paste), dissolved in 1 tbsp of water (optional)

METHOD

1. Finely grind ingredients of the paste. (If grated coconut is unavailable, add coconut milk to the curry towards end of the cooking time.)

2. Add paste to a pan and roast. When it is aromatic, add water.

3. Heat mixture. Add sliced onions, fenugreek seeds, pounded garlic, turmeric powder and salt. Bring to boil. Lower heat and simmer for 3-4 minutes.

4. Add fish pieces gently to boiling curry.

5. Continue to simmer till flesh of the fish is white and cooked. Add curry leaves, then tamarind water and coconut milk (if using).

6. Simmer for another minute or so. Remove from heat and serve with rice or other staple.

IRAAL KARI

Prawn Curry / *Tightly curled prawns in a sea of warm coconut milk, with green chillies, fennel and fenugreek.*

PREPARATION TIME: 20 MIN
COOKING TIME: 30 MIN
SERVINGS: 3-4

INGREDIENTS

500 g medium-large prawns
1 cup coconut milk
3 tbsp oil
1 medium onion, sliced finely
4 cloves garlic, sliced
1 green chilli, slit lengthways and cut into pieces
½ tsp fenugreek seeds
1 tsp fennel seeds
4 tsp curry powder
Salt (to taste)

METHOD

1. Clean prawns. Discard shells, heads and tails. Wash and set aside to dry.
2. Heat oil in a pan or wok. Add fenugreek seeds and fennel seeds, then sliced onions, sliced garlic and green chillies. Add curry powder.
3. Sauté mixture until onions are translucent.
4. As onions start to change colour, add prawns. Stir well and cover.
5. Cook over a gentle heat for 3-5 minutes until prawns are curled and cooked.
6. Add coconut milk and salt to taste. Mix well, then cover and cook for a further 3 minutes.
7. Uncover and stir well. When curry has thickened, remove from heat and serve with rice or other staple.

KOLI KARI

Chicken Curry / The intense flavours in this curry are delicately balanced with coconut milk, and its fire tempered with lemon. It is a wholesome dish, which can be shared over rice, idiappam or puttu.

PREPARATION TIME: 20 MIN
COOKING TIME: 20 MIN
SERVINGS: 4

INGREDIENTS

500 g boneless chicken pieces

2 green chillies (or to taste)

6 cloves garlic

3 cm piece ginger, chopped finely

1 tsp oil

2 medium onions, sliced

½ tsp fenugreek seeds

1 sprig curry leaves

¼ cup water

1½ tsp salt (or to taste)

2 tsp curry powder

1 cup coconut milk

1 tsp garam masala

Juice ½ lemon or lime

METHOD

1. Pound green chillies, garlic and ginger together.
2. Heat oil in a pan over medium heat. Gently fry half the sliced onions, pounded mixture and fenugreek seeds.
3. Add curry leaves.
4. Add chicken pieces, then water and salt. Cover and cook over medium heat until chicken is nearly cooked through.
5. Add curry powder. Mix well and continue to cook uncovered.
6. Add remaining onions and coconut milk, stirring constantly to avoid burning.
7. Reduce heat when almost cooked and add garam masala.
8. Sprinkle with lime or lemon juice and mix well again.
9. Remove from heat and serve warm, with rice or other staple.

Garam Masala: Equal parts of fennel seeds, cardamom, cinnamon and cloves are dry-roasted and then ground.

MANJAL
TURMERIC (YELLOW GOLD)

"Manjal (yellow) in colour, pavun (gold) in its benefits," says Easwari, 60 years of age.

Manjal (turmeric) belongs to the ginger family. Turmeric roots are used fresh or dried and ground, and turmeric is used generously in Sri Lankan food for its taste and colour and also for its medicinal properties.

"When we had a bad cough, our mother would boil a little milk, add turmeric powder, kalkandu (sugar crystals) and a pinch of ground black pepper and make us sip this twice a day. I used to love it, but my brother could not stand the manjal and pepper together."

Turmeric has anti-inflammatory properties and aids in the relief of arthritic pain in the joints; its anti-bacterial and anti-fungal properties make it beneficial in the treatment of skin disorders, and it is used an antiseptic to treat cuts and burns.

It is also used as a beauty treatment – Easwari's mother would grind *kasturi manjal* with water and make her smear it all over her face and hands. *"She said it would keep my face clear of blemishes. I did it, but I did not like the strange yellow tinge it left on my face after I had washed it off."*

Turmeric is closely connected with ritual and ceremony in Sri Lanka and India. On auspicious occasions, a white cotton cloth is dyed with turmeric as a symbolic clearing of the space and an invitation to the gods. Often Ganesha, *Aanai Mugathaan*, the Elephant-Faced One and Remover of Obstacles, is invited to this ceremony through the symbolic presence of a small ball of turmeric paste.

With its earthy aroma and taste, its ubiquitous presence in the everyday as well as the occasional turmeric occupies an honoured place in the home. Harvested for its gastronomic properties, it's as if it nourishes the body with its therapeutic benefits as it reaches symbolically to the heavens to invoke the gods.

PREPARATION TIME: 15 MIN
COOKING TIME: 20 MIN
SERVINGS: 4

INGREDIENTS

500 g large firm fish (e.g., mackerel, tuna)

½ cup grated coconut

½ tsp turmeric powder

½ tsp salt

1 tsp oil

3 small onions, sliced finely

1 green chilli, slit lengthways and cut into pieces

½ tsp fennel seed powder, dry-roasted

1 sprig curry leaves

1 tsp lime juice (optional)

METHOD

1. Clean and cut fish into 4 cm cubes.
2. Place fish in a pan and add enough water to cover. Boil till fish turns white and is cooked through.
3. Remove fish from water and place in a bowl. Remove bones and skin if desired.
4. Mix together grated coconut, turmeric powder and salt. Add to the fish and mix gently so that fish is smeared with mixture and pieces stay intact.
5. Heat oil over medium heat in a frying pan. Add sliced onions and when they turn translucent, add chilli.
6. Add fish and toss gently to mix.
7. Add fennel seed powder. Mix again. After a minute or so, add curry leaves.
8. Remove from heat and add lime juice to give it a tang and eliminate any fishy smell.
9. Serve with rice or other staple.

MEEN VARAI

Fish Fry /

Delicately fried pieces of fish, coated in morsels of coconut, thick with the taste of curry leaves, turmeric and sweet fennel seeds.

SURAA VARAI

Shredded Milk Shark Fry /

Fleshy strands of fish coated in a coconut sea of spices, dotted with little islands of chillies, red and green.

PREPARATION TIME: 10 MIN
COOKING TIME: 15 MIN
SERVINGS: 4

INGREDIENTS

500 g milk shark pieces (paal suraa), gummy shark or flake fillets

½ cup water

½ cup grated fresh coconut

1 tsp chilli powder

10 small rose onions (or 3 medium onions), sliced

5 green chillies, chopped (or 5 whole dried red chillies)

1 sprig curry leaves

1 tsp fennel seeds

2 tbsp coconut oil (or as required)

Salt (to taste)

METHOD

1. Poach milk shark pieces in water. When the flesh turns white and is cooked remove them. Set aside to cool.
2. Mix grated coconut with chilli powder and set aside.
3. When shark pieces have cooled, mash with fingers, removing skin and bones. It should have a flaky, shredded appearance.
4. Add coconut oil to a frying pan. When hot, add onions, green chillies, curry leaves and fennel seeds. When onions turn a light golden-brown, add mashed shark. Toss gently over low heat.
5. Add coconut with chilli powder. Mix well, turning over and over and adding salt to taste. Toss until the salt is mixed through and the dish has the texture of shredded coconut.
6. Remove and serve.

A *varai* is a dry preparation of vegetables or seafood served as an accompaniment to rice. It usually – but not necessarily – contains freshly grated coconut.

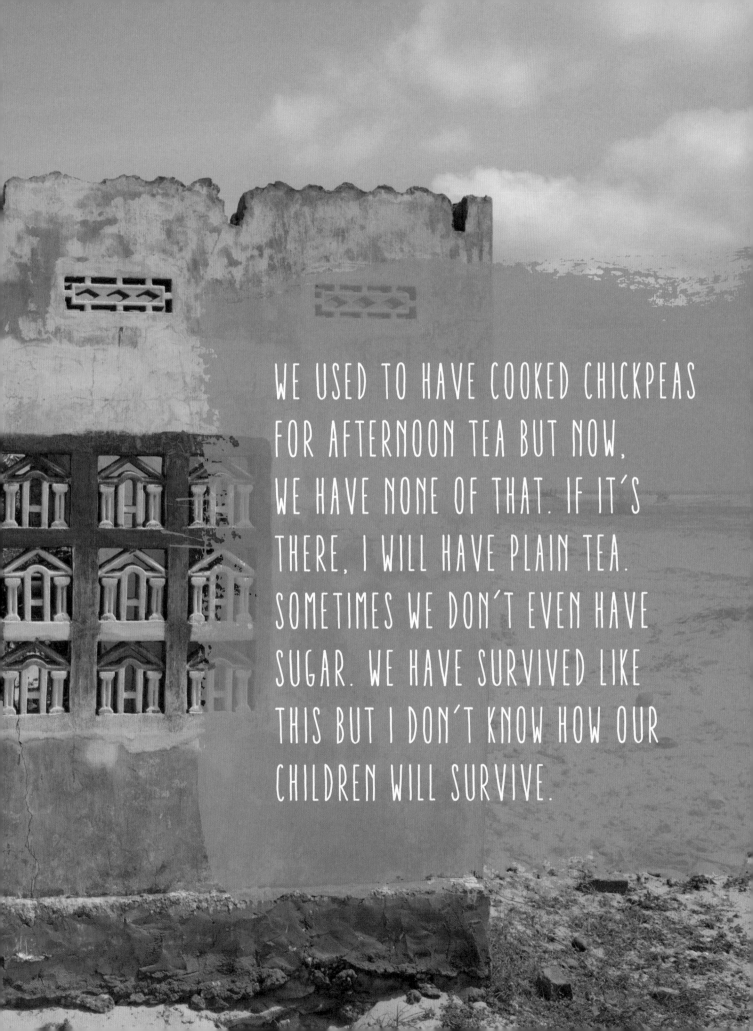

WE USED TO HAVE COOKED CHICKPEAS FOR AFTERNOON TEA BUT NOW, WE HAVE NONE OF THAT. IF IT'S THERE, I WILL HAVE PLAIN TEA. SOMETIMES WE DON'T EVEN HAVE SUGAR. WE HAVE SURVIVED LIKE THIS BUT I DON'T KNOW HOW OUR CHILDREN WILL SURVIVE.

INGREDIENTS

500 g squid, cleaned and sliced

6 cloves garlic, pounded

2–3 cm piece fresh ginger, pounded

¼ tsp turmeric powder

2 tsp chilli powder

4 tsp oil

3 green chillies, slit lengthways and cut into pieces

1 sprig curry leaves

1 medium onion, sliced

½ tsp salt

METHOD

1. Marinate pieces of squid in garlic, ginger, turmeric and chilli powder. Set aside for at least half an hour.
2. Heat oil, add pieces of squid, cover and allow to cook for 5-7 minutes, stirring occasionally.
3. When almost cooked, add green chillies, curry leaves, onion and salt. Cook uncovered, stirring continuously to avoid burning and until the gravy is almost dry.
4. Remove from heat and serve hot.

PREPARATION TIME: 30 MIN
COOKING TIME: 15 MIN
SERVINGS: 4-6

Fried Squid / *The earthy aroma of curry leaves meets the sea in this dry squid preparation, against a backdrop of turmeric, punctuated with ginger, garlic and green chillies.*

KANAVAAI PORIYAL

Asaiva Odiyal Kool

Uppu Kanji (Kanji Thanni)

Saamai Kanji

Uluththamma Kool

Aadi Kool

SOUPS AND WARMERS

PREPARATION TIME:
45 MIN
COOKING TIME: 25 MIN
SERVINGS: 4-6

INGREDIENTS

2 cups palmyra root flour
(odiyal maa)

150 g firm fish

150 g shelled prawns

1 small crab (150 g), cleaned
and cut into small pieces

100 g long beans, chopped roughly

1 medium cassava, peeled and cut
into small pieces

8-10 jackfruit seeds (remove outer
skin and cut each seed in half)

8-10 dried chillies, ground

2-3 cm piece turmeric root
(or 1 tsp turmeric powder)

1 tsp cumin seeds

½ tsp pepper powder

6 medium cloves garlic, crushed

½ tbsp cooked rice

½ cup drumstick
(murungakkai) leaves

4 tbsp tamarind water (mix ½ tbsp
tamarind paste in 4 tbsp water)

2 tsp salt (to taste)

ASAIVA ODIYAL KOOL

Palmyra Root Flour Seafood Chowder / A hearty,
transparent broth that tastes of all the fish in the sea...
thickened with the creamy, fibrous texture of palmyra root.
It is popular in the coastal areas of the north and east of
Sri Lanka, where seafood is readily available.

REQUIRED
» Strainer
» Muslin cloth to line the strainer

METHOD
1. Cut fish, prawns, crab and vegetables into bite-sized pieces and set aside.
2. Place odiyal flour in a bowl and cover with water, then drain water. Repeat this at least three times to reduce the bitterness (if odiyal flour has been freshly ground this process may not be necessary). Finally, pour flour into a strainer lined with muslin cloth. Draw edges together and squeeze out the excess water. Set aside.
3. Coarsely grind dried chillies, cumin, turmeric and garlic cloves together. Set aside.
4. In a saucepan, place 2 cups water, seafood and vegetables. Cook on low heat for a few minutes until seafood is cooked.
5. Add another 2 cups of water to odiyal flour and mix well.
6. Add odiyal flour mixture to saucepan, stirring constantly with a wooden spoon to prevent lumps forming.
7. Dry-roast chilli, cumin, turmeric and garlic mixture and pepper. Add this mixture to the saucepan with seafood, vegetable and odiyal flour mixture. Add cooked rice.
8. Add tamarind water and drumstick leaves. Add salt to taste.
9. Keep stirring gently till flour is cooked and chowder thickens. Remove from heat and serve hot.

Kool, an odiyal flour-based soup, is quintessentially Sri Lankan Tamil. It is a rich and nutritious dish, eaten on social occasions. Traditionally, the kool pot would be placed in the centre of the group. Cleaned and polished half-coconut shells (kottaangachi or thengai chirattai) – would be used as bowls to drink the chowder. Sometimes jackfruit leaves would be fashioned into a cone to make a 'spoon' to drink it. It is difficult to beat the ecstasy of slurping kool from a kottaangachi!

UPPU KANJI
(KANJI THANNI)

PREPARATION TIME: 15 MIN
COOKING TIME: 25 MIN
SERVINGS: 4

INGREDIENTS

¼ cup long-grain rice (red or white), parboiled rice, or broken rice
1½ litres water
3 cloves garlic, finely chopped
1 cm slice fresh ginger
1 tsp ground peppercorns
¼ cup coconut milk
Salt (to taste)

METHOD

1. Crush uncooked rice in a mortar and pestle or use 'pulse' action in a food processor to break the rice to a rough texture. Broken rice needs no grinding.
2. Place rice, garlic and ginger in a saucepan and cover with water. Boil till rice practically dissolved in water (it should look like cloudy water).
3. Simmer for further 2-3 minutes.
4. Add ground pepper and/or coconut milk if desired.
5. Remove from heat and add salt to taste. Mix well and serve hot.

Savoury Rice Porridge /

A restorative dish, filled with goodness despite being so light. Uppu kanji is often prepared to strengthen a person in times of ill health. It is usually paired with a spicy accompaniment like a pickle or chutney.

Saami Rice Porridge / *Rough, tough saamai 'rice' is boiled and boiled again, along with smooth, soporific coconut milk, producing a warm, filling porridge. It is pronounced 'saami kanji'.*

SAAMAI KANJI

COOKING TIME: 1 HR
SERVINGS: 4

INGREDIENTS

1 cup saamai rice ('little millet')

3 cups water

Salt (to taste)

½ cup coconut milk

1 tbsp sugar (if desired)

METHOD

1. In a saucepan, bring water to boil. Meanwhile, wash and drain saamai rice.
2. When water has boiled, add rice and salt. Stir frequently while cooking.
3. When rice is cooked (overcooked, really!) to a mushy, porridge-like consistency, add coconut milk. Stir and bring to boil again.
4. Add sugar if desired and stir till dissolved. Remove from heat. Serve warm.

Visalakshi strokes her daughter's frizzy black hair. The 11-year-old sits quietly, nestling into the comfort of her mother's shoulder. Visalakshi's eyes grow distant as she recalls the 12 months she moved from camp to camp with her husband, daughter and son. The children were constantly asking for *thosais*, *puttu* and other starch-based foods. She tugs on the girl's plait as she remembers the pain she felt when she could not give them this.

Kamakshi interrupts her mother to remind her of the gram (lentil) flour that was boiled every evening. Visalakshi grimaces and adds that gram flour was in no short supply. *"It was boiled every evening and served on its own. I used to feel nauseated when I inhaled the smell of the steaming flour."*

Now, three years on, she has returned to her home and the children are back at school. Eager to provide them with nutritious food each morning, she often serves them uluththamma kool, a sweet rice porridge. Although its texture is reminiscent of food in the camps, the luxurious ingredients of coconut and jaggery make it truly special. She boils the rice and dhal and grinds them before adding the coconut milk and pieces of jaggery. Even during the months of drought, when coconut and jaggery are unavailable, she continues to prepare the dish but with other more readily available pulses and flours.

ULUTHTHAMMA KOOL

Sweet Rice Porridge / *Caramel brown in colour, with flecks of white coconut – tasting somewhere in between sweet and salty, with a dash of pepper and cumin to warm.*

PREPARATION TIME: 10 MIN
(+ SOAKING)
COOKING TIME: 35 MIN
SERVINGS: 4

INGREDIENTS

1 cup parboiled rice, soaked at least 2 hours

2 cups water

2 tsp green gram (paasipayaru), roasted

5 tsp fresh coconut, chopped small

⅔ cup jaggery, powdered

2 cups water (in addition to above)

¼ cup coconut milk

2 tsp black gram flour (uluththammaa), dry roasted

1 tsp salt

¼ tsp pepper

¼ tsp cumin powder

METHOD

1. Drain soaked rice and grind it. Do not add water.
2. Take about a quarter of ground rice and set aside.
3. In a saucepan, bring 2 cups water to boil.
4. Add roasted green gram, coconut and rice set aside.
5. In another pan, mix 2 cups of water, remaining ground rice and jaggery.
6. Boil until jaggery is fully dissolved, then remove from heat and pour into other pan of rice and green gram.
7. Mix the dry roasted black gram flour in the coconut milk. Add this mixture to the pot. Lower the heat and keep stirring to prevent lumps.
8. Bring to boil and add salt, pepper and cumin powder. Stir well.
9. Remove from heat and serve warm.

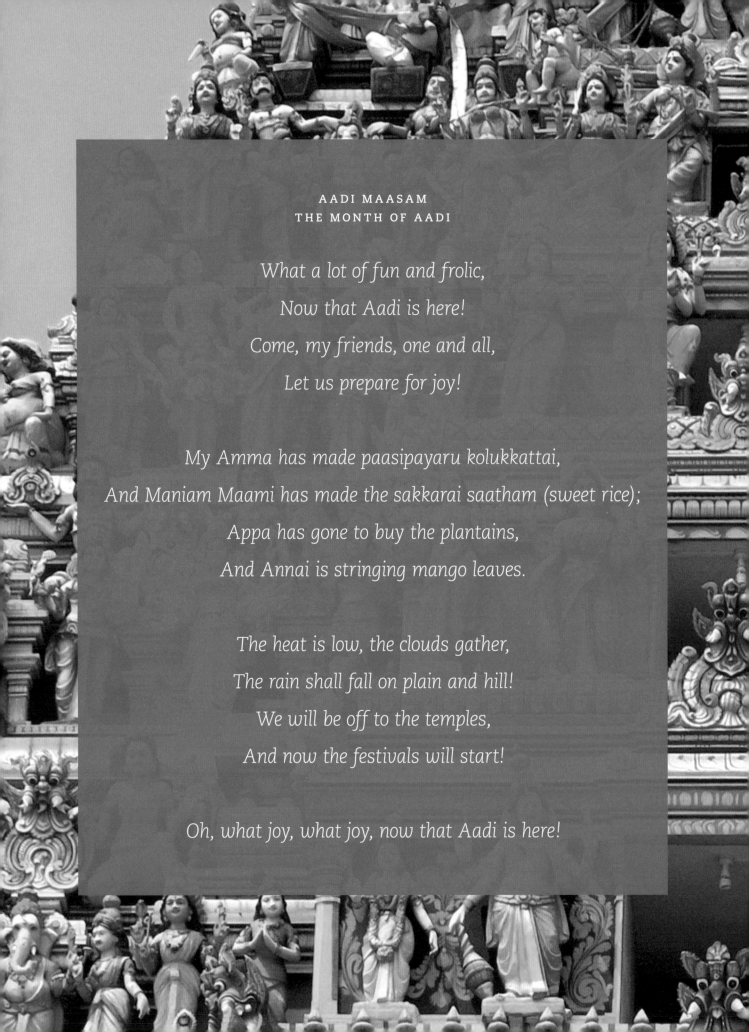

AADI MAASAM
THE MONTH OF AADI

What a lot of fun and frolic,

Now that Aadi is here!

Come, my friends, one and all,

Let us prepare for joy!

My Amma has made paasipayaru kolukkattai,

And Maniam Maami has made the sakkarai saatham (sweet rice);

Appa has gone to buy the plantains,

And Annai is stringing mango leaves.

The heat is low, the clouds gather,

The rain shall fall on plain and hill!

We will be off to the temples,

And now the festivals will start!

Oh, what joy, what joy, now that Aadi is here!

Nanthini sings a ditty heard long ago, punctuating the song with her claps and laughter. The other women – *ammas*, *akkas* and aunties – join in, clapping and singing under their breath. It sums up the significance of *Aadi*, an auspicious time in the Tamil calendar from mid-July to mid-August. With the coming of *Aadi*, the oppressive heat of summer abates and the cool monsoon rains start.

Now is the season of festival after festival, in temple, town and home. Mariamman (the mother goddess) and Murugan (the handsome, youthful god who rides a peacock) are invoked and worshipped. The pilgrim path to the Murugan temple in Kataragama, where in legend he married Valli the hunter girl, is crowded. Devotees bring offerings of fruit, flowers and sweet items to the deity and follow with a picnic lunch in the temple precinct.

Aadi also heralds the sowing season after the fields have been flooded by the generous monsoon. People entreat the gods for a fruitful harvest and good health to reap the bounty. In anticipation, families cook *aadi kanji* and *aadi kool*, sitting together and slurping the sweet broths.

Yes, finally, Aadi is here. Nanthini has prepared *kolukkattai* and *sakkarai saatham* and, after offering some to Lord Murugan, cannot wait to share it with her neighbour, Kalaichelvi.

AADI KOOL MARKS AN OCCASION

Aadi is the fourth month in the Tamil calendar. It is an auspicious time for Hindus, heralding a two-month-long celebration of temple festivals and religious days. Parasakthi used to enjoy making foods that marked this season. Her face comes alive with expression and her hands begin moving as she reminisces about the *kool* she used to prepare as a breakfast treat for her husband. She would get up early to boil the rice and *dhal*; and pick a coconut from the almost infinite supply on her garden floor. She would stir the grated coconut, *jaggery*, cumin and salt until there were no lumps. Her husband was always delighted to wake to this breakfast and would gulp down two or three bowls full.

Her lips begin to quiver as she describes the outbreak of fighting and the displacement that followed. That year, *Aadi* was not marked by the ringing bells of the temple, but by flying shrapnel and the sound of shells drumming the earth.

For a while now, she and her husband have not had work and are struggling to provide their family with regular meals. Parasakthi focuses her time and energy on making the most of the ingredients she comes across, experimenting with them and substituting them for the traditional ones. With this creativity, her meals are a surprise and a treat, making a celebration of the everyday.

Sweet Porridge for the Month of Aadi / *A warm, luxurious treat to awaken to in the mornings of the month of Aadi.*

AADI KOOL

PREPARATION TIME: 1 HR
COOKING TIME: 40 MIN
SERVINGS: 8

INGREDIENTS

2 tsp black gram (ulunththu), split, skinless, and soaked for an hour

2 tsp green gram (paasipayaru), split

2 cups water

¼ cup jaggery, powdered

½ cup tiny fresh coconut pieces

3 cups coconut milk

1 cup rice flour

¼ tsp salt (or to taste)

METHOD

1. Boil black gram and green gram in a saucepan with water.
2. When cooked, add jaggery and coconut pieces. Stir well and lower heat. Cook till jaggery is dissolved.
3. In a bowl, mix coconut milk, rice flour and salt.
4. Keeping heat low, add coconut mixture slowly to saucepan, stirring to avoid lumps. Keep stirring for a smooth texture.
5. When well cooked, remove from heat and serve warm.

SWEETS

Muttai Maa

Kootu Maa

Ariyatharam

Paiththam Urundai

Inippu Thosai

Sakkarai Rotti

Thothal (Dodol)

Paal Tofi

Panang-kali Seththa Arisi-Maa Neiappam

Rasavalli-kilangu Kali

Uluthang Kali

Ravai Biskut

Ellu Pahu

Idiappa Kolukkattai

MUTTAI MAA

Egg, Rice and Black Gram Flour Meal / *Flours of rice and black gram combine in this nutritious sweet, lightly flavoured with cardamom and sesame, with the smoothness of egg as a binder.*

PREPARATION TIME: 1 HR
COOKING TIME: 30 MIN
SERVINGS: 4

INGREDIENTS

1 cup rice flour

3 tbsp milk (or as required)

2 medium eggs

¼ cup sesame (gingelly) oil

4 tsp ghee

½ cup black gram flour (uluththammaa)

2 tbsp white sugar (or caster sugar)

½ tsp cardamom powder (or vanilla essence)

METHOD

1. Dry-roast rice flour till grainy to the touch. Separately, dry-roast black gram flour.
2. Beat eggs lightly in a bowl. Set aside.
3. After rice flour has cooled, add milk and stir into a grainy paste or dough. Add a little more milk if necessary.
4. Place gingelly oil and ghee in a heavy-based pan, over medium heat. When hot, lower heat.
5. Add rice flour dough and eggs. Stir together briskly over low heat.
6. Keep turning mixture over to prevent burning.
7. As it turns golden, add roasted black gram flour and sugar.
8. Continue turning mixture over and over constantly so it cooks evenly. When golden and dry, add cardamom powder. Mix thoroughly, and then remove from heat.
9. When cool, store in an airtight container.

A precious recipe passed from mothers to daughters, it is packed with nutrition and given to girls through puberty and during pregnancy, to build their strength. Mothers sent airtight containers of this snack with their children when they left home to study in the capital Colombo, or to India. This was the basis of their nutrition when away from their mother's care.

PREPARATION TIME: 5 MIN
COOKING TIME: 10 MIN
SERVINGS: 4-6

INGREDIENTS

1 cup black gram (ulunththu), split and skinless

½ cup broken rice

½ cup green gram (paasipayaru), split and skinless

½ cup yellow lentils (kadalai paruppu), split

½ cup peanuts, skinless and roasted

½ cup white sesame seeds

½ cup grated coconut

1 cup sugar

½ cup maize (corn) kernels (optional)

METHOD

1. In a heavy-based pan, place black gram, broken rice, green gram, yellow lentils and maize kernels (if using). Dry-roast over low heat, stirring, until fragrance of roasted grains emerges, and they begin to turn golden. Remove from heat.
2. Place grain mixture in a grinder with peanuts and sesame seeds. Grind coarsely.
3. Place this mixture in a bowl, and add coconut and sugar. Mix well.
4. When cool, store in a clean, airtight container.

KOOTU MAA

Rice, Corn and Lentil Meal / *This finely-ground sweet snack contains a nutritious mixture of black gram, split yellow lentils, green gram, rice, peanuts and sesame seeds.*

WE'VE GOT TO BE GRATEFUL TO GOD FOR ALL THAT IS GIVEN TO US. SOME FAMILIES HAVE NO FATHER; OTHERS HAVE NO MOTHER AND OTHERS HAVE NEITHER. WE ALL HAVE PROBLEMS BUT WE MUST MOVE ON.

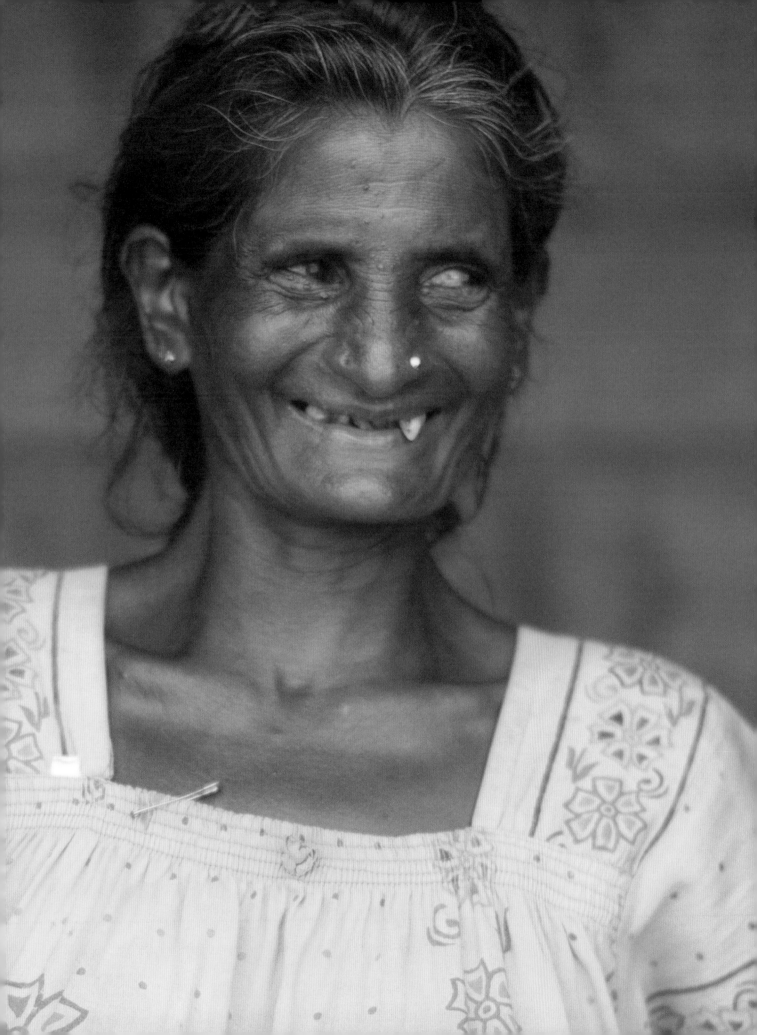

ARIYATHARAM

Ground Rice Sweet /

These golden balls have a crisp outer shell and a soft inner. The thick, doughy taste of rice is infused with a hint of sesame and the rich taste of ghee.

Great when eaten warm, and just as good a day later. *Ariyatharam* is very much a treat for festive occasions and no *palaharam* tray at a wedding or a *samathiyachadangu* (coming of age ceremony for a young girl), would be complete without it.

This sweet is often made and served at the conclusion of a matrimonial match. Made of rice flour and sugar, it is served in the hope of sustaining sweetness in the relationship.

PREPARATION TIME: 15 MIN (+ SOAKING)
COOKING: 30 MINS
MAKES: 25-30

INGREDIENTS

2 cups rice, soaked overnight

1 tsp salt

1 tsp sesame seeds

2 tbsp ghee, melted

1 cup sugar

⅓ cup water

Oil for deep-frying

METHOD

1. Drain soaked rice – it should be as dry as possible. Grind finely in food processor or grinder. Remove any large bits and place in a bowl.

2. Add salt, sesame seeds and ghee. Mix well and set aside.

3. In a saucepan, make a thick sugar syrup: boil sugar with ½ cup water over very low heat, stirring constantly until sugar is completely dissolved and mixture forms a soft ball consistency. (When you drop a little syrup into a cup of water it should form a soft ball and not disintegrate.) Remove from heat.

4. Pour syrup into rice mixture and mix well to form a dough.

5. Let dough sit for about 3 hours, until it becomes firm.

6. Mix dough again to refresh it. Form into 25-30 little balls. Flatten each ball slightly to form a disc.

7. Heat oil. Deep-fry balls and remove when they change to a light golden colour at the edges. Over-frying will make the ariyatharam hard.

8. Cool and serve.

Green Gram Balls / Soft, ochre-yellow balls, coated in a bright, fried yellow covering. These little balls look like small suns, shielding an earthy sweetness inside, with specks of freshly grated coconut.

PAITHTHAM URUNDAI

PREPARATION TIME: 25 MIN
COOKING TIME: 35 MIN
MAKES: 20

INGREDIENTS

125 g green gram (paasipayaru) flour

125 g red rice flour

100 g grated coconut (fresh or frozen)

60 g brown sugar

60 g white sugar

½ tsp cardamom powder

60 g plain flour

¼ tsp turmeric powder

¼ tsp salt

Water

Coconut oil

METHOD

1. Roast green gram flour lightly. Mix with rice flour.
2. Over low heat, dry-roast grated coconut to a light golden colour. Remove and set aside.
3. In a large bowl, place roasted coconut, brown sugar, white sugar, green gram flour and red rice flour, and cardamom powder. Mix well. Add a little water to moisten mixture enough to form little balls with your hands.
4. Make little balls of approximately 3 cm diameter. Make sure balls are firm. Set aside.
5. Make a batter with plain flour, turmeric powder and salt. Add water until batter drips from your fingers in a thick, smooth and steady stream.
6. Heat oil until very hot. Dip each ball into batter and drop gently into hot oil. Do not put in too many at once as they may stick together. Cook until they are a light golden colour.
7. Drain on a tray lined with absorbent paper or newspaper and cool.
8. Serve, or store in an airtight container until ready to serve.

PREPARATION TIME: 30
(+ FERMENTATION)
COOKING TIME: 25 MIN
MAKES: 12

INGREDIENTS

3½ cups plain flour

1 tsp baking powder

1 egg

¼ tsp salt

Water

2 cups grated coconut

½ cup sugar

½ cup brown sugar

REQUIRED

» A thosai pan or a medium-sized frying pan

METHOD

1. In a bowl, mix plain flour and baking powder.
2. Make a well in centre and add egg and salt. Mix with a wooden spoon.
3. Add enough water to make a pancake-like batter.
4. Set batter aside for 3 hours.
5. After 3 hours, stir batter again.
6. Heat and grease a thosai pan or frying pan. Spread a thin layer of mixture over pan and fry thosai until it turns light golden. Repeat with rest of batter. Set stack of pancakes aside.
7. In a bowl, mix grated coconut, sugar and brown sugar.
8. Place a spoonful of sweet coconut mixture in centre of each thosai and fold thosai into a 'pocket' or roll, with coconut mixture inside.
9. Serve warm.

INIPPU THOSAI

Sweet Thosai /

The delicate, light thosai pancake folds onto itself, enclosing a spoonful of juicy, sweet coconut.

Brown Sugar Rotti / *Coconut milk and brown sugar form a rich, dark, complex sweetness; while rice flour adds fineness to the texture and green gram a coarser dimension. These rottis can be eaten for breakfast or, due to their ability to keep, can be eaten as a wholesome snack on a journey.*

SAKKARAI ROTTI

COOKING TIME: 1 HR
SERVINGS: 4

INGREDIENTS

2 tbsp green gram (paasipayaru)

½ cup light coconut milk

½ cup brown sugar (if using jaggery, powder it first)

½ cup small bits fresh coconut

1 tbsp rice flour, very lightly dry-roasted

½ tsp cardamom powder

Oil or ghee

REQUIRED

» Idiappa steamer (avikrer chatti) or alternative steamer
» Banana leaf or baking paper

METHOD

1. Dry-roast green gram. Remove from heat.
2. Bring about ½ cup water to boil in a saucepan. Add roasted green gram. Boil till soft. Drain and set aside.
3. In another saucepan, boil coconut milk and brown sugar till sugar has dissolved.
4. Add cooked green gram and coconut bits. Mix well.
5. Add rice flour a little at a time to mixture, stirring constantly with a wooden spoon to prevent lumps forming.
6. Continue stirring until ingredients are well combined. Remove from heat and set aside to cool.
7. Once cool to the touch, form dough into balls about the size of a lime.
8. Grease tray of steamer and line with a piece of banana leaf or baking paper.
9. Bring water to boil in steamer.
10. Grease a palm-sized piece of banana leaf or baking paper. Place a ball of dough on it and flatten to about 1 cm thick. Make a hole in centre of '*rotti*', like a doughnut.
11. Slide *rotti* from the banana leaf onto the steamer tray. Put lid on and steam '*rotti*' till cooked. Serve warm.

Rice Flour Slice / Everyone's thothal (dodol) tastes different, but some aspects prevail: the dark, shiny squares of a soft, slightly rubbery texture; the full, sweet taste that smothers the palate and the slightly oily fingers that remain, searching for another piece.

PREPARATION TIME: 15 MIN
COOKING TIME: 20 MIN
MAKES: 25

INGREDIENTS

5½ cups thick coconut milk

¾ cup rice flour

½ cup plain flour

½ tsp salt

2½ cups jaggery or brown sugar

½ tsp cardamom powder

50 g roasted cashew nuts, chopped small

METHOD

1. Mix rice flour, plain flour, salt and jaggery in 2 cups of coconut milk.
2. Bring remaining coconut milk to boil in a large pot or wok.
3. Add flour mixture, stirring continuously till mixture leaves sides of pan.
4. With a spoon, skim off any excess oil as it emerges from the coconut milk.
5. Add cardamom powder and cashew nuts.
6. Turn off heat. Turn mixture out onto a greased tray and flatten like a slice. When cool (after about 1 hour), cut into squares and serve. Thothal can be stored in an airtight container for a week or so.

THOTHAL

WHEN MY CHILDREN ASK ME TO BUY FOOD THAT THEY LIKE, I USUALLY TELL THEM THAT I WILL BUY IT LATER WHEN WE HAVE MORE MONEY. IT PAINS ME THAT I CAN'T BUY THE THINGS THAT MY CHILDREN ASK ME FOR.

Milk Toffee / *Sightings of milk toffee generally mean that a festive occasion is near, or has just passed. For this reason this soft, caramel-coloured sweet is powerful as a traditional symbol of festivity and joy.*

COOKING TIME: 1 HR
MAKES: 20

INGREDIENTS

1 can condensed milk
Water (¼-½ volume of condensed milk)
Handful cashew nuts
1 cup sugar
2 tbsp butter
1 tsp vanilla essence

METHOD

1. Grease tray with edges for spreading the toffee.
2. Dry-roast cashew nuts. Remove from heat and crush into small pieces using a mortar and pestle.
3. In a heavy-bottomed pan (preferably non-stick), add condensed milk, water and sugar. Mix well.
4. Cook mixture on medium heat, stirring constantly with a wooden spoon.
5. As mixture thickens, add butter and vanilla essence and keep stirring. The mixture will thicken further and begin to leave sides of pan. Keep stirring for another couple of minutes.
6. Remove mixture from heat and pour into greased tray. Spread with a spatula or butter knife.
7. Allow to cool slightly before cutting into bite-sized squares. Do not let it cool for too long: toffee becomes very hard to cut once completely cool.
8. When cool break up squares and serve. Toffee can be stored in an airtight container for a week or so.

PAAL
TOFI

PANAI MARAM

THE PALMYRA PALM (A WISH-FULFILLING TREE)

The palmyra is a tree that offers every part of itself for use: its bark for fuel, its leaves for shelter and its fruit for food.

It is the veritable gift-giving tree that abounds in South India, Sri Lanka and South-East Asia. It stands tall, intrinsically symbolic of the landscape, houses, livelihoods and food of people in the north and east of Sri Lanka. Its leaves are fashioned into hundreds of useful items, from toys to winnowing trays; its trunk is used to build fences and walls covered with leaf thatching, and its fruit is eaten in various forms.

Karuppani (more formally *pathaneer*), a sweet nectar, is extracted from the flowers of the male tree. It is drunk as is, or with tiny bits of green mango in it. Fresh *karuppani* is a good source of Vitamin B complex. The *karuppani* is boiled to make *jaggery*, the dark brown sugar in sweet dishes. *Jaggery* is more nutritious than crude cane sugar, containing small traces of protein, fat, minerals, calcium and phosphorus, copper and iron. *Karuppani* is often fermented into the sweet-sour alcoholic drink known as *toddy* or *kallu*, which is often used to ferment the rice flour mixture for *appam*.

The pulp of the ripened *palmyra* fruit is made into many sweet dishes. Traditionally, the ripe fruit is cooked in embers, peeled and the pulp is extracted from the fibres. The fibres, laden with golden pulp, are then pressed through a colander. The thick liquid is then strained again through a sieve or coarse muslin to extract the smooth *panang-kali* (*palmyra* pulp). Many lovers of the *palmyra* slurp up the juice from the fibres themselves, the golden liquid dripping around their mouths!

The fruit has three fruit 'eyes'; this is the clear jelly-like *nongu*, eaten whole with great relish, or sliced into rings in a drink. The three seeds of the fruit are planted in specially prepared ground. After a couple of months, the saplings are lifted out. The roots are cut off, washed and the thick skin peeled. The white root is dried to make *pulukkodiyal*, a hard snack. The dried roots are ground to make *odiyal* flour. This flour is prized to make *puttu* and chowders like *odiyal maa kool*.

Cans of *palmyra* pulp are sold in Indian, Sri Lankan and Asian grocery stores around the world. The standard packaging belies the potency and majesty of its original life-giving source.

PANANG-KALI SETHTHA ARISI-MAA NEIAPPAM

Palmyra Pulp and Rice Sweet /

Palmyra pulp – bright orange and yellow, like a liquid sun dripping thickly, is churned with brown sugar, pounded rice and coconut milk. It is cooked in a kuli paniyaaram pan to form golden balls of sweetness, around a dull bitterness from the palmyra.

PREPARATION TIME: 1 HR
(+ SOAKING)
COOKING TIME: 20 MIN
MAKES: 12

INGREDIENTS

½ cup palmyra fruit pulp

¼ cup sugar, brown or white

1 cup long-grain rice, soaked for 2 hours

Salt (to taste)

½ tsp baking soda

½ cup thick coconut milk

Oil (or ghee)

REQUIRED

» A kuli paniyaaram mould or tray with circular depressions that can be placed over heat

METHOD

1. Place palmyra pulp and sugar in a saucepan. Cook over medium heat, stirring constantly to prevent lumps or burning, until sugar has dissolved.
2. Remove from heat and set aside to cool.
3. Drain soaked rice and grind in a food processor into a rough-textured flour. It is important for the flour to have a granular texture. Remove from food processor and set aside.
4. Add the wet, ground rice to saucepan of palmyra pulp and sugar.
5. Add salt and baking soda. Mix well.
6. Add coconut milk and mix well. Place back over heat. Stir continuously till mixture has a thick porridge-like consistency. Remove from heat and allow to cool for at least 2 hours.
7. When mixture has cooled, place kuli paniyaaram pan on heat.
8. Add ¼ tsp oil or ghee in each little depression.
9. Drop a spoonful of neiappam batter into each depression of the utensil, three-quarters of the way up to allow room for rising. When cooked, remove with a fork and serve warm.

Rajini vividly recalls Pallai, a lush, green land, rich with vegetables – thick, furry, lime-coloured okra; glossy black and green egglplant; and an abundance of purple yam. The vegetable she still treasures from those days is rasavalli-kilangu, the humble looking one. Rajini used to enjoy the purple yam season: watering, watching and waiting for the yams to grow. When they were ready, she happily picked and pruned the tubular yams, peeling a few for the upcoming weeks, and preserving a handful for the months ahead. The yams would last up to 6 months after picking.

She uses the *rasavalli* to make a *kali*, a simple and nutritious breakfast porridge. Her mother taught her how. She leans forward to explain how she peels, dices and then cooks the yam until it is soft enough to mash. Her hands launch into a mashing motion. She explains that it can be boiled with coconut milk or cow's milk, depending on your preferred texture and taste. Coconuts, in short supply because of the drought in Kilinochchi, are too expensive, so she uses cow's milk now. Her 5 growing children don't mind this substitution, though she remembers the creamy coconut version.

Rajini believes her children perform better at school when their tummies are full. She says they are more lively in the mornings and able to concentrate better. To be able to adapt this traditional dish to her current circumstances, and contribute to her children's happiness and wellbeing brings her great satisfaction and joy.

PREPARATION TIME: 10 MIN
COOKING TIME: 20 MIN
SERVINGS: 6-8

RASAVALLI-KILANGU KALI

Purple Yam Pudding / *The purple yam is cooked till tender, its colour muted by the addition of thick, white coconut milk to yield a luxuriously soft porridge.*

INGREDIENTS

500 g purple yam, peeled and diced (frozen yam can be substituted)

Water, to cover yams

1 cup thick coconut milk

⅓ cup sugar

½ cup water

½ tsp salt

½ tsp vanilla essence

METHOD

1. Rinse yam pieces a few times to remove any sticky residue.
2. Place yams in saucepan with enough water to cover them. Cook till soft and drain water.
3. Lower heat. Mash yam while in the pot.
4. Add coconut milk, water, sugar and salt. Mix thoroughly and turn off heat.
5. Add vanilla essence and mix well.
6. Remove from saucepan and serve warm.

ULUTHANG KALI

Black Gram and Rice Flour Cream / *Smooth in texture, this kali (meaning clay) is fine in texture but substantial. Fawn in colour with the addition of jaggery, it tastes predominantly of rice and coconut, grounded by the pithy addition of black gram. It is often served with sesame oil stirred through.*

COOKING TIME: 40 MIN
SERVES: 4–6

INGREDIENTS

¼ cup black gram flour (uluththamma),
purchased already roasted

1 cup rice flour

¼ tsp salt

½ cup light coconut milk

½ cup jaggery (or sugar)

½ cup coconut milk

METHOD

1. Dry-roast black gram flour. Let it cool.
2. Off heat, place black gram flour, rice flour, salt and light coconut milk in a saucepan. Mix well removing any lumps.
3. Place saucepan over medium heat and bring mixture to boil, stirring continuously. The mixture will begin to thicken.
4. Add jaggery.
5. Lower heat. Add thicker coconut milk and keep stirring till mixture reaches a thick mousse-like consistency.
6. Remove from heat and set aside to cool. Serve warm or cold – every mouthful full of goodness!

"It is the very best thing to give our girls when they attain age."

Their mothers and grandmothers were given *uluthang kali* and *nallaennai* (sesame oil) when they attained age, continuously for a few days. *"Perhaps that is why we have had the strength to survive these ordeals."* The women in the group nodded in passionate agreement.

Semolina Biscuits / *Smooth, spongy semolina biscuits are packed densely with raisins and cashews. The ingredients are basic and the cooking simple; though this is called a 'biscuit', it is almost like a cake.*

RAVAI BISKUT

PREPARATION TIME: 15 MIN
COOKING TIME: 30 MIN
MAKES: 20-25

INGREDIENTS

250 g fine semolina

50 g butter or margarine

125 g sugar

¼ cup raisins

¼ cup chopped cashew nuts

3 small eggs

METHOD

1. Pre-heat oven to 180°C.
2. Place semolina, margarine or butter, sugar, raisins and chopped cashew nuts in a bowl. Mix well.
3. Beat eggs in a bowl.
4. Add to semolina mixture. Mix well.
5. Pour into a lined cake tray.
6. Score lines to form bite-sized squares on the surface.
7. Bake 30 minutes or until golden and firm to the touch.
8. When cool, cut into scored squares and serve.

GINGELLY OIL (SESAME OIL)

"Vaithi-yaanu-ku kuduk-kura kaasai, vaaniyaanukku kudu," old Parameswary tells us: The money you would give to the doctor, give to the oil-monger. *"What that nallennai has, no medicine has!"* she says, flinging her hands in front of her and leaning back in her chair.

Nallennai, the 'good oil' she speaks of is gingelly oil, extracted from sesame seeds. This is the oil that has sustained the health of her family and her people.

Gingelly oil deserves its reputation. It has been used for centuries in Ayurveda for therapeutic massages. The oil is absorbed readily into the skin, drawing out impurities and improving circulation. It is used in the weekly 'oil bath' that is part of the lives of Tamils, both in India and Sri Lanka. The oil acts as a barrier to the harmful effects of UV rays and it is quite common to see men and children covered in this 'good oil' sitting on mats in the sun for a couple of hours. The hot bath that follows removes the oil and lowers the body temperature, leaving the body fresh and cool in the heat of the day.

Babies enjoy a massage with the oil, as their limbs are toned and strengthened. It keeps joints supple and protects the tender skin from rashes. The oil has anti-bacterial and anti-fungal properties, and is used in the treatment of skin conditions such as Psoriasis and Athlete's foot.

Pressed from the sesame seed, *gingelly* oil is used in *ellu pahu* (sesame sweet), and in nutritious snacks like *muttai maa* (sweet rice and egg pancake) and *kootu maa* (mixed grain snack) especially prepared for girls going through puberty, for nursing mothers and for recovering patients.

Gingelly oil has a high smoking temperature and can be used for deep-frying. It is best used in stir-fries, and imparts a nutty flavour. It is also a 'good' oil because it has been known to maintain and increase the 'good' cholesterol (HDL) and reduce the 'bad' cholesterol (LDL).

"It is truly a nallennai," says Parameswary, stroking the wrinkled but soft and supple skin on her arms.

Sesame Balls / *Delicate sesame seeds are ground up, their oil drawn out to infuse the dark, rich sweetness of jaggery. Grandmothers would make these balls and store them in a jar and children would be given one each.*

ELLU PAHU

PREPARATION TIME: 45 MIN
MAKES: 10-15

INGREDIENTS
250 g white sesame seeds

125 g jaggery

METHOD
1. Wash sesame seeds and dry well.
2. Pound sesame seeds in a mortar and pestle till they ooze oil. Add jaggery and pound further to form a smooth mixture.
3. Form mixture into small balls about size of a lime.
4. Store balls in a jar, pouring any extra sesame oil over top. These balls can be kept for well over a week.

"All the goodness of sesame and the oozing gingelly oil will keep the doctors out of work," chuckled an elder.

IDIAPPAM KOLUKKATTAI

String Hopper and Coconut Parcels / *A sweet, grainy mixture of coconut and jaggery, enveloped in a half-moon of fragile, stringy idiappam and steamed to fuse the taste of the components.*

PREPARATION TIME: 10 MIN
COOKING TIME: 5 MIN
SERVINGS: 12-15

INGREDIENTS

12-15 fresh idiappam (string hoppers, red or white rice) (see page 123)

2 cups grated coconut

1 cup powdered jaggery or brown sugar

½ tsp ground cardamom

REQUIRED

» Baking paper or banana leaf

METHOD

1. Mix together coconut, jaggery and cardamom powder in a bowl. Set aside.
2. Take one idiappam and spoon a little of sweet coconut mixture on one half of the circle. Fold other half over to form a crescent shape. Repeat process with all the idiappa. Alternatively, take one idiappam, top it with filling and use another idiappam on top to sandwich the filling. Repeat process with remaining idiappa.
3. Line a steamer with banana leaf or baking paper.
4. Carefully place idiappa on steamer and steam (in batches) till no longer sticky to the touch.
5. Serve warm.

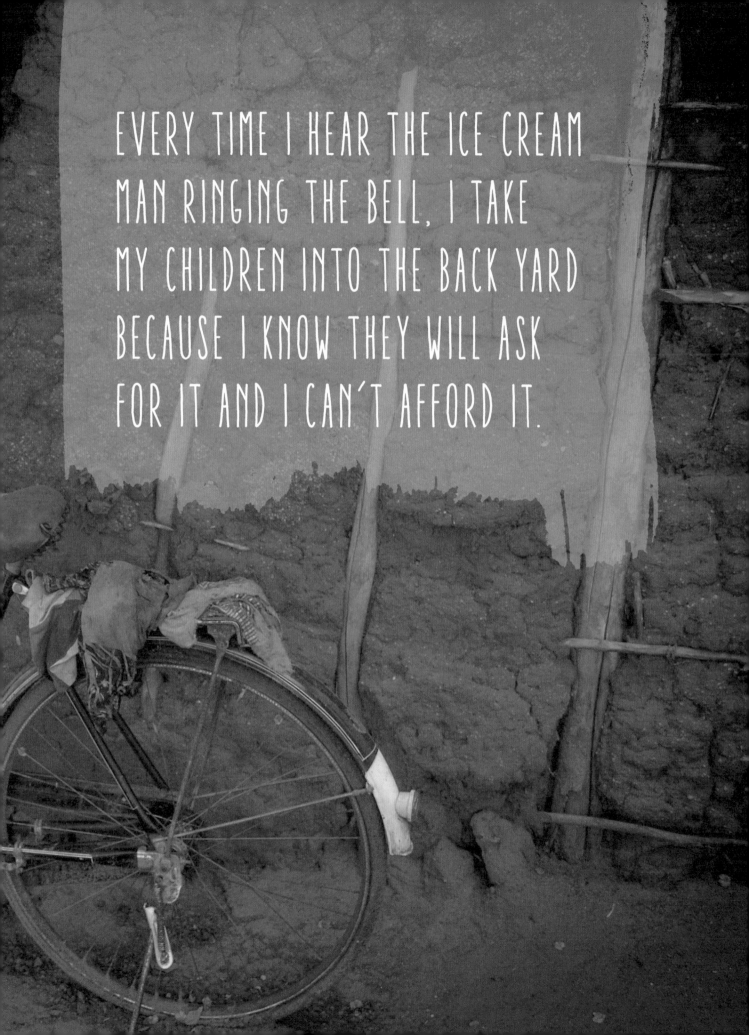

EVERY TIME I HEAR THE ICE CREAM MAN RINGING THE BELL, I TAKE MY CHILDREN INTO THE BACK YARD BECAUSE I KNOW THEY WILL ASK FOR IT AND I CAN'T AFFORD IT.

DRINKS

Thesikkai Saaru

Mor Thanni

Masala Thethanni

Malli Thanni

THESIKKAI SAARU

Fresh Lime Juice (Sweet) /
*A morning spent under the gaze of
a scorching sun. A parched throat.
There is nothing like stumbling upon
a vendor on the street, or wandering
into a home and being greeted with
a glass of this refreshing drink. A bit
like finding an oasis in the desert.*

**PREPARATION TIME:
10 MINS
SERVINGS: 4**

INGREDIENTS

8 limes

4 glasses water

2 tsp salt

4 tsp sugar (to taste)

METHOD

1. Cut limes in half and squeeze.
2. Add water, salt and sugar.
3. Serve as is or refrigerate
   before serving.

PREPARATION TIME: 10 MIN
MIXING TIME: 5 MIN
SERVINGS: 4

INGREDIENTS

1 cup unsweetened yogurt

½ tsp asafoetida powder (optional)

Salt (to taste)

4 cups water

1 green chilli, chopped finely

½ red onion, chopped finely

1 tsp coriander leaves, chopped finely

1 tsp oil

1 tsp mustard seeds

1 sprig curry leaves

Lemon juice (to taste)

METHOD

1. Mix yoghurt with asafoetida powder (if using) and salt.
2. Dilute yoghurt mixture with water, to an easy-drinking consistency.
3. Add green chillies, onion and coriander leaves to yoghurt mixture.
4. Heat oil. Roast mustard seeds and curry leaves. When mustard seeds splutter, remove from heat and add to yoghurt mixture.
5. Add lemon juice to taste.
6. Serve straight away!

MOR THANNI

Spiced Yoghurt Drink / *On a hot day, this flavoursome blend of yoghurt and spices goes down well, cooling the body and replenishing its salts.*

Masala Tea / *There's nothing like a spiced tea to refresh you, morning or evening – at home or on the street. This recipe is to tea what 'chukku (ginger) kopi' and 'malli (coriander) kopi' are to coffee.*

PREPARATION TIME: 5 MIN
COOKING TIME: 10 MIN
SERVINGS: 4

INGREDIENTS

2¼ cups water

4 black tea bags (or 4 tsp tea granules)

1 whole star anise, pounded

1 stick cinnamon, pounded

4 cardamom pods, cracked

¼ cup sugar

2 cups milk

METHOD

1. In a saucepan, lightly roast star anise, cinnamon and cardamom.
2. Add water, tea bags or tea granules and milk and bring mixture to boil. Turn heat down and allow it to bubble for a few minutes.
3. Strain tea into cups. Add sugar if desired.

MASALA THETHANNI

THE NATURAL ENERGISER

Leela, a young mother of two, sits still in her chair. Still, like a bird,
but alert, ready to fly at any moment. Her fingers are interwoven and placed firmly
on her batik cloth purse. She speaks in an even tone as she recounts her pregnancy
and the birth of her daughter, in the camps that she was moved to after the war.

Unlike her first pregnancy, this time her mother was not by her side feeding
her *kanjis* (soups), teas and confinement foods throughout the day. In the camp,
at times she even went without meals for a few days.

One day, she remembered the reassuring taste of *malli thanni*, a tea of boiled
coriander seeds, peppercorn and ginger that her mother used to prepare.
Leela managed to accumulate enough coriander seeds during her visits to the
doctor outside the camps. Whenever she felt weak or had not eaten, she prepared
this concoction. She also fed it to her young son who was often afflicted with colds
throughout their time in the camps.

*Leela says how thankful she was for the
magic coriander seeds that kept her energised
for the birth of her daughter.*

KUDI NEER
OR MALLI THANNI

Coriander Water / When the monsoons sweep into Sri Lanka and South India, comfort drinks packed with healing properties are prepared. This is an intense concoction that women swear by. Its clear, sharp taste warms the body, warding off colds, and in times of scarcity, tides the body over till the next source of nourishment.

COOKING TIME: 15 MIN
SERVINGS: 3

INGREDIENTS

⅔ cup coriander seeds

9 or 10 black peppercorns

2-3 cm piece fresh ginger, sliced or pounded

3 cups water

Sugar (optional)

METHOD

1. Place coriander seeds and peppercorns in a heavy-bottomed saucepan. Dry-roast over low heat. As the aroma rises, remove from heat.
2. Add ginger and water to coriander seeds and peppercorns. Bring to boil.
3. Reduce heat and simmer till liquid is considerably reduced, to half or less.
4. Add sugar if desired, and stir to dissolve. Simmer for another 4-5 minutes on low heat.
5. Remove from heat. Serve warm for relieving a cold or cool as a wellbeing tonic.

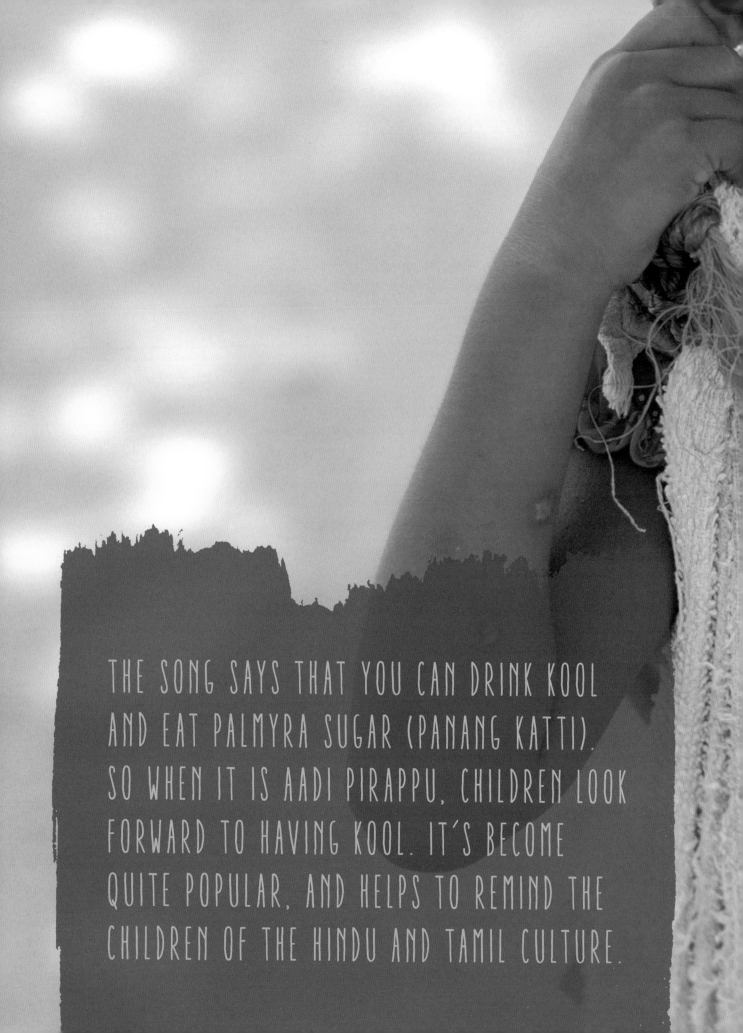

THE SONG SAYS THAT YOU CAN DRINK KOOL AND EAT PALMYRA SUGAR (PANANG KATTI). SO WHEN IT IS AADI PIRAPPU, CHILDREN LOOK FORWARD TO HAVING KOOL. IT'S BECOME QUITE POPULAR, AND HELPS TO REMIND THE CHILDREN OF THE HINDU AND TAMIL CULTURE.

PALMERA

Palmera works with the women featured in this book, in micro-enterprises through the north and east of Sri Lanka. These are stories of women who have stepped out from their homes to be leaders in their community.

Palmera is a tree that can be found in the heart of villages in Sri lanka. Every part of the tree is used to serve, the bark for fuel, the leaves for shelter and the fruit for food.

Our goal is to enable communities to work collectively to achieve livelihood security and a thriving village economy.

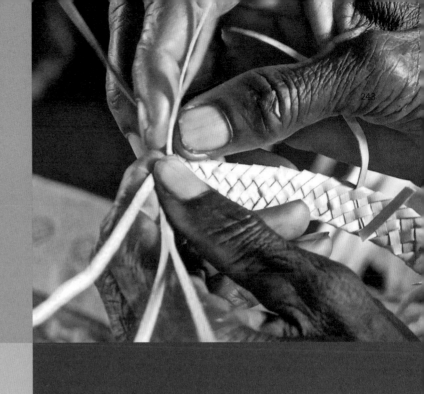

We work with smallholder farmers and rural entrepreneurs, first sparking their desire. Bringing a market-based approach to their village ecosystem, we facilitate activities at various stages of small enterprise development including training, financing and market generation through networking and mentorship.

We see confidence growing, income secured, and lives improved in lasting ways. Importantly, with social cohesiveness at the heart of our approach, the village economy thrives.

We believe that we move the dial from dependence to dignity and allow the journey of self-sufficiency to begin.

palmera.org

PAPAYAS

She is a small-scale farmer in Vavuniya, and like many others in her village she relies on her farm to earn an income. However, the local market prices can be volatile and with limited access to wider markets, sometimes she doesn't have enough money to meet her family's daily needs.

Sparked by her desire to grow, we are working with her to cultivate papayas allowing her to diversify production and serve a new international market.

This is a big step for Thangarini but she has a new vision for her farm and now a determination to achieve it.

We have been working with Thangarini and 29 other farmers to support them through the changes; from training on the new crop variety, to setting up a drip irrigation system for water conservation, and providing the rights tools. With the stability of these supports, farmers can now build connections to the international market.

"We never thought that we would be able to save water like this. This new water system is very important for us and it is very easy to use. Let me show you."

GOATS

Arumuham recalls the thriving goat-rearing industry in her village in Kilinochchi, before the war.

Sparked with a desire to be self-sufficient and with a clear vision in their minds, we supported the women of the village as they reacquainted themselves with skills of building shelters, managing the goats' feed and monitoring their health. We mentored them in building networks with the local veterinary hospital and connecting with local buyers. This support is preparing Arumuham to meet challenges of growing and securing her business and ensuring her sustainability.

She now has a fresh and plentiful supply of milk which give her children a nutritious start each morning. Proudly, Arumuham points to the cool, thatch shelter she built where the newborn goats are resting:

"You know, my son loves these goats. He has them to play with when I am busy working."

CHICKENS

On a cleared patch of land behind untamed shrubs in a small village in Mulathivu, a poultry farm houses over 150 chickens. It all began with the group's idea for a community-run business focused on poultry farming. It was a response to market demand, their skills and the food security challenges they faced.

We provided business members with intensive training on poultry farming, start-up capital and strategic support to grow the enterprise. Trees have been planted, fences have been built, and in just 12 months the farm is generating food, employment and income. The 35 entrepreneurs have a vision not only for their farm, but also for their community and they are eager for the next phase of growth.

But running a poultry farm of this size is not easy and they work day and night to ensure the chickens are well fed and healthy:

"Do you know that if you feed them too much they die? If you feed them too little they die. If you feed them at the wrong time they die. Actually, it is easy for them to die and hard for them to stay alive!"

The farmers all burst into laughter. For those involved, it is clear, the time is now.

PALMYRA

The women gather in the heat of the day, in the district of Vavuniya. Weaving together gives them a chance to work with the materials they have a deep affinity for, whilst providing respite from the sun. It is also the way they decided to diversify their income.

We supported them to plan their business, providing training in weaving and product design, in understanding the market and in marketing their wares. Since then have built retail connections with the local market and Mannar, a nearby coastal village.

Over the course of the day, objects of the woven palmyra leaf emerge. A square coaster with intricate geometric patterns; circular discs, with a splash of purple or bright pink on the edge.

We are working with these women to grow their micro-business so they can sell their products in major cities in Sri Lanka and the world. Having seen their business grow, and now with the possibility of expansion, the women continue to chat excitedly as they realise just what may be possible.

GLOSSARY

Almost all these ingredients are available in Indian, Sri Lankan or Asian grocery stores in most major cities of the world. Many dry ingredients may even be purchased online.

APPAM

Hoppers. Rice flour pancakes with a deep, soft centre, and crispy outer layer.

ASAFOETIDA

Tamil: *perungaayam*. Extracted from sap exuded by the root of a plant in the fennel family, asafoetida is a pungent spice that adds a savoury element to food. Widely used in Indian cooking, particularly in vegetarian dishes, it can be sourced as a hard resin block or in powdered form. It has a strong smell that disappears in the cooking process. It is used in curries, *rasams* (light, spicy broth), and with lentils as a digestive aid.

BROKEN RICE

Rice grains that are broken during the milling process.

CURRY LEAF

Tamil: *karuvepillai*. An aromatic leaf from the curry tree which is native to Sri Lanka and India. It is often used in Sri Lankan cuisine for aroma and sometimes aroma. Curry leaves are also used as a herb in Ayurvedic medicine and are believed to possess anti-diabetic properties.

FENNEL SEEDS

Tamil: *perunjeeragam*. The dried seeds of the fennel plant. Their aromatic flavour makes them a popular addition to curries. Fennel seeds are added to food or offered after a meal as a mouth freshener and for their carminative properties, warding off flatulence.

FENUGREEK SEEDS

Tamil: *venthayam*. The dried seeds of the fenugreek plant are commonly used in the Indian subcontinent, particularly for tempering in fish curries. They are recommended for diabetics because they slow down sugar absorption and aid the production of insulin. Nursing mothers are given fenugreek seeds in their food to increase the flow of milk.

GHEE

Tamil: *ney*. Clarified butter. Used extensively in Indian and Sri Lankan cuisine.

GINGELLY OIL

Tamil: *nalla ennai*, shortened to *nallennai*. Oil extracted from sesame seeds. See feature on page 220.

IDIAPPAM String hoppers. Plural: *idiappa*. Clumps of fine, rice flour noodles steamed and served with a curry and or chutney.

IDLI Steamed rice flour cakes. A breakfast staple usually accompanied by a *sambar* (lentil curry) and a coconut chutney or *sambal*.

IRAAL Prawns.

JAGGERY Tamil: *panangkatti*. Brown sugar made from boiling the sweet liquid tapped from the male flowers of the palmyra palm. Considered to be more nutritious than processed cane sugar.

KAARAI Chilli.

KADALAI PARRUPU Yellow lentils. Also called bengal gram and *toor dhal*.

KAAJU Cashew nuts.

KOLUKKATTAI A dumpling or parcel filled with a sweet filling.

KOOL A soup or porridge.

KURAKKAN *Raagi* or 'finger millet'. This lean grain belongs to the 'millet' group of cereals. *Kurakkan* flour is used to make *rottis*, *puttu* and gruels.

MARAVALLI-KILANGU Cassava. The cassava plant is a woody shrub, and its root is often mistakenly referred to as a yam. Starchy cassava root is dried and powdered into tapioca, called *mandioca* in many South American countries, where it is widely eaten. Cassava root can also be cubed and cooked as a curry or sliced thinly and fried into chips. The tapioca flour is made into 'pearls' and used in puddings and the delightful dessert porridge called *paayasam* in Indian cooking. Tapioca pearls are called *savvarasi* in Tamil.

MURUNGAKKAI Drumstick. Also known as *murunggai*. These young seed pods of the *moringa oleifera* tree resemble sticks, hence the name. See feature on page 138.

252

MUSTARD SEEDS

Tamil: *kadugu*. The tiny seeds of the mustard plant, which belongs to the Brassicaceae (cruciferous) family (along with broccoli, brussels sprouts and cabbage). Rich in selenium and magnesium, they are used in Indian and Sri Lankan cooking for tempering curries and stir-fries. They may be black, yellow or white. Mustard oil is also used in cooking.

PALAHARAM

Sweet and savoury snacks like *laddus*, *murukku* and *vadais*, prepared on special occasions.

PALMYRA PALM

Tamil: *panai maram*. A tall palm with fan-shaped leaves, commonly found in India, Sri Lanka and South-East Asia. All parts of the palm are used, especially its flowers and fruit. See feature on page 209.

PALMYRA PULP

Tamil: *panang-kali*. Inside its fibrous coating, the palmyra fruit is densely filled with a thick, golden liquid, or pulp. This pulp is extracted after cooking the fruit in embers to soften it. It is used in sweets and puddings.

PALMYRA ROOT

Tamil: *pulukkodiyal*. The seeds of the palmyra fruit are planted in specially prepared soils. When the saplings are about three and a half months old, they are uprooted. The main roots are cut off, washed, and the thick outer sheaths are removed. These are dried in the sun till they shrivel and harden. This is called *pulukkodiyal*. It is chewed as a snack or ground into flour.

PALMYRA ROOT FLOUR

Tamil: *odiyal maa*. Flour ground from palmyra root (*pulukkodiyal*).

PARBOILED RICE

Tamil: *pulungal arisi*. Also called 'idli rice'. When the husk is removed, leaving the bran on the grain it is called brown rice. When this is further 'polished' to remove the bran, it becomes white rice. For parboiled rice, the whole grain of rice in its husk is soaked, steamed and dried, then the husk is removed. In this process, the nutrients are moved into the endosperm (body) of the grain, so the rice retains its nutrients. Parboiled rice is a far healthier option than white rice as it retains high quantities of Vitamin B6 and minerals. It has a low glycemic index compared to white rice and is an excellent choice for diabetics as it prevents blood sugar spikes.

PORIYAL	A dry, stir-fried or deep-fried dish.	**SAMBA RICE**	Tamil: *samba arisi*. Rice grown in Sri Lanka and in South India. It is more oval in shape than long-grain rice. It is also more starchy than long-grain rice and is an acquired taste.
PUTTU	A staple of rice flour and coconut steamed into a cylindrical cake often referred to as *pittu* in Sri Lanka. It is served at breakfast time with a curry.	**SAMBAL**	A generic name for a spicy side-dish accompanying *appam* or *idiappa*, often containing coconut, combined with chilli and onion.
RASAVALLI-KILANGU	Purple yam. A yam (*dioscorea alata*) with light to dark purple flesh; not to be confused with taro or sweet potatoes. It is used to make a sweet porridge.	**SAMBAR**	A lentil curry that is an accompaniment to staples of *idli*, *thosai*, *puttu* and rice.
RAVAI	Semolina.		
ROSE ONIONS	Tamil: *chinna vengaayam*. As the name suggests, these are small, round, red onions. They are more pungent than white onions or shallots. They are sometimes used whole in curries.	**SESAME SEEDS**	Tamil: *ellu*. Sesame seeds are black (with the skin on) or white (when husked). They are exceptionally nutritious and yield a rich 50% of oil from seed. Sesame oil or *nallaennai* (gingelly oil in India) has a wide range of therapeutic benefits including lowering cholesterol, inhibiting sugar absorption in diabetics, and nourishing skin, among others.
ROTTI	A thin, flat bread, and a staple of India, Sri Lanka and Malaysia. Rottis are made from wheat flour and come in many shapes, sizes and thicknesses, and may include oil.		
		SOTHI	A gravy accompaniment for *idiappam* and other staples, made with vegetables in a base of coconut milk.
SAAMAI RICE	Tamil: *saamai arisi*. This is a small yellowish rice, and when cooked looks like cous cous.		

SUNDAL	A generic name for a dry preparation of lentils.
TAMARIND	Tamil: *puli*. Tamarind is used in cooking for its delightful tangy taste. The sweet-tangy flavour enhances *rasams* and fish curries. It can be purchased as a thick paste, seeds and all, and then dissolved in water and strained for use. Tamarind concentrate and thick tamarind water are also available. In Asian cooking, vinegar is sometimes used as a substitute for tamarind in pickles and curries.
TAPIOCA	See **Cassava root**.
THAKKAALI	Tomato.
THOSAI	Pronounced *thosé*. A thin rice-flour pancake, usually served for breakfast and accompanied by a *sambar* and/or coconut chutney or *sambal*.

ULUNTHTHU	Black gram. Also called *urad dhal*. A lentil rich in vegetable protein, it can be purchased whole with the skin on, or skinless and split. It is used extensively in Sri Lankan cuisine for its nutritious compounds.
VADAHAM	A fritter or deep-fried preparation.
VADAI	Pronounced *vadé*. A fried, lentil snack with many variations.
VEPPAM	Margossa and/or neem. An evergreen, shady tree belonging to the mahogany family, it has been called 'the village pharmacy', for its medicinal value. See feature on page 61.
VER KOMBU	Tamil: *chukku*. Dried ginger root. It is used in coffee and other preparations to aid digestion and comes in a powdered form.

Concept by **Abarna Suthantiraraj**
Recipes written by **Nesa Eliezer**
Stories written by **Anjali Roberts**
Edited by **Jessica Perini**
Publication coordinated by **Sivanjana Kathiravel**
Designed by **Shruti and Frank Thiruchelvam,
Pink Tank Creative**

THERE'S A STORY
IN HER HANDS